THE MAN AGAINST THE SKY
THE TOWN DOWN THE RIVER
THE MAN WHO DIED TWICE

THE MACMILLAN COMPANY
NEW YORK · BOSTON · CHICAGO · DALLAS
ATLANTA · SAN FRANCISCO

MACMILLAN & CO., LIMITED
LONDON · BOMBAY · CALCUTTA
MELBOURNE

THE MACMILLAN CO. OF CANADA, LTD.
TORONTO

COLLECTED POEMS

THE MAN AGAINST THE SKY
THE TOWN DOWN THE RIVER
THE MAN WHO DIED TWICE

By EDWIN ARLINGTON ROBINSON

THE MACMILLAN COMPANY

NEW YORK   MCMXXVII

PS
3500
R659
1927
v.2

SET UP AND ELECTROTYPED BY T. MOREY & SON

PRINTED IN THE UNITED STATES OF AMERICA BY
THE BERWICK & SMITH CO.

The author begs to acknowledge his indebtedness to Messrs. Charles Scribner's Sons for permission to include in this collection the contents of the volume entitled "The Town Down the River."

CONTENTS

THE MAN AGAINST THE SKY
(1916)

To the Memory of
William Edward Butler

FLAMMONDE

The man Flammonde, from God knows where,
With firm address and foreign air,
With news of nations in his talk
And something royal in his walk,
With glint of iron in his eyes,
But never doubt, nor yet surprise,
Appeared, and stayed, and held his head
As one by kings accredited.

Erect, with his alert repose
About him, and about his clothes,
He pictured all tradition hears
Of what we owe to fifty years.
His cleansing heritage of taste
Paraded neither want nor waste;
And what he needed for his fee
To live, he borrowed graciously.

He never told us what he was,
Or what mischance, or other cause,
Had banished him from better days
To play the Prince of Castaways.
Meanwhile he played surpassing well
A part, for most, unplayable;
In fine, one pauses, half afraid
To say for certain that he played.

For that, one may as well forego
Conviction as to yes or no;
Nor can I say just how intense
Would then have been the difference
To several, who, having striven
In vain to get what he was given,
Would see the stranger taken on
By friends not easy to be won.

Moreover, many a malcontent
He soothed and found munificent;
His courtesy beguiled and foiled
Suspicion that his years were soiled;
His mien distinguished any crowd,
His credit strengthened when he bowed;

[2]

And women, young and old, were fond
Of looking at the man Flammonde.

There was a woman in our town
On whom the fashion was to frown;
But while our talk renewed the tinge
Of a long-faded scarlet fringe,
The man Flammonde saw none of that,
And what he saw we wondered at—
That none of us, in her distress,
Could hide or find our littleness.

There was a boy that all agreed
Had shut within him the rare seed
Of learning.   We could understand,
But none of us could lift a hand.
The man Flammonde appraised the youth,
And told a few of us the truth;
And thereby, for a little gold,
A flowered future was unrolled.

There were two citizens who fought
For years and years, and over nought;

They made life awkward for their friends,
And shortened their own dividends.
The man Flammonde said what was wrong
Should be made right; nor was it long
Before they were again in line,
And had each other in to dine.

And these I mention are but four
Of many out of many more.
So much for them.   But what of him—
So firm in every look and limb?
What small satanic sort of kink
Was in his brain?   What broken link
Withheld him from the destinies
That came so near to being his?

What was he, when we came to sift
His meaning, and to note the drift
Of incommunicable ways
That make us ponder while we praise?
Why was it that his charm revealed
Somehow the surface of a shield?
What was it that we never caught?
What was he, and what was he not?

How much it was of him we met
We cannot ever know; nor yet
Shall all he gave us quite atone
For what was his, and his alone;
Nor need we now, since he knew best,
Nourish an ethical unrest:
Rarely at once will nature give
The power to be Flammonde and live.

We cannot know how much we learn
From those who never will return,
Until a flash of unforeseen
Remembrance falls on what has been.
We've each a darkening hill to climb;
And this is why, from time to time
In Tilbury Town, we look beyond
Horizons for the man Flammonde.

THE GIFT OF GOD

Blessed with a joy that only she
Of all alive shall ever know,
She wears a proud humility
For what it was that willed it so,—
That her degree should be so great
Among the favored of the Lord
That she may scarcely bear the weight
Of her bewildering reward.

As one apart, immune, alone,
Or featured for the shining ones,
And like to none that she has known
Of other women's other sons,—
The firm fruition of her need,
He shines anointed; and he blurs
Her vision, till it seems indeed
A sacrilege to call him hers.

She fears a little for so much
Of what is best, and hardly dares
To think of him as one to touch

With aches, indignities, and cares;
She sees him rather at the goal,
Still shining; and her dream foretells
The proper shining of a soul
Where nothing ordinary dwells.

Perchance a canvass of the town
Would find him far from flags and shouts,
And leave him only the renown
Of many smiles and many doubts;
Perchance the crude and common tongue
Would havoc strangely with his worth;
But she, with innocence unwrung,
Would read his name around the earth.

And others, knowing how this youth
Would shine, if love could make him great,
When caught and tortured for the truth
Would only writhe and hesitate;
While she, arranging for his days
What centuries could not fulfill,
Transmutes him with her faith and praise,
And has him shining where she will.

She crowns him with her gratefulness,
And says again that life is good;
And should the gift of God be less
In him than in her motherhood,
His fame, though vague, will not be small,
As upward through her dream he fares,
Half clouded with a crimson fall
Of roses thrown on marble stairs.

THE CLINGING VINE

"Be calm?   And was I frantic?
    You'll have me laughing soon.
I'm calm as this Atlantic,
    And quiet as the moon;
I may have spoken faster
    Than once, in other days;
For I've no more a master,
    And now—'Be calm,' he says.

"Fear not, fear no commotion,—
    I'll be as rocks and sand;
The moon and stars and ocean
    Will envy my command;
No creature could be stiller
    In any kind of place
Than I . . . No, I'll not kill her;
    Her death is in her face.

"Be happy while she has it,
    For she'll not have it long;
A year, and then you'll pass it,
    Preparing a new song.

And I'm a fool for prating
　　Of what a year may bring,
When more like her are waiting
　　For more like you to sing.

"You mock me with denial,
　　You mean to call me hard?
You see no room for trial
　　When all my doors are barred?
You say, and you'd say dying,
　　That I dream what I know;
And sighing, and denying,
　　You'd hold my hand and go.

"You scowl—and I don't wonder;
　　I spoke too fast again;
But you'll forgive one blunder,
　　For you are like most men:
You are,—or so you've told me,
　　So many mortal times,
That heaven ought not to hold me
　　Accountable for crimes.

"Be calm? Was I unpleasant?
    Then I'll be more discreet,
And grant you, for the present,
    The balm of my defeat:
What she, with all her striving,
    Could not have brought about,
You've done. Your own contriving
    Has put the last light out.

"If she were the whole story,
    If worse were not behind,
I'd creep with you to glory,
    Believing I was blind;
I'd creep, and go on seeming
    To be what I despise.
You laugh, and say I'm dreaming,
    And all your laughs are lies.

"Are women mad? A few are,
    And if it's true you say—
If most men are as you are—
    We'll all be mad some day.
Be calm—and let me finish;

There's more for you to know.
I'll talk while you diminish,
    And listen while you grow.

"There was a man who married
    Because he couldn't see;
And all his days he carried
    The mark of his degree.
But you—you came clear-sighted,
    And found truth in my eyes;
And all my wrongs you've righted
    With lies, and lies, and lies.

"You've killed the last assurance
    That once would have me strive
To rouse an old endurance
    That is no more alive.
It makes two people chilly
    To say what we have said,
But you—you'll not be silly
    And wrangle for the dead.

"You don't? You never wrangle?
    Why scold then,—or complain?

More words will only mangle
    What you've already slain.
Your pride you can't surrender?
    My name—for that you fear?
Since when were men so tender,
    And honor so severe?

"No more—I'll never bear it.
    I'm going.   I'm like ice.
My burden?   You would share it?
    Forbid the sacrifice!
Forget so quaint a notion,
    And let no more be told;
For moon and stars and ocean
    And you and I are cold."

CASSANDRA

I heard one who said: "Verily,
　　What word have I for children here?
Your Dollar is your only Word,
　　The wrath of it only your fear.

"You build it altars tall enough
　　To make you see, but you are blind;
You cannot leave it long enough
　　To look before you or behind.

"When Reason beckons you to pause,
　　You laugh and say that you know best;
But what it is you know, you keep
　　As dark as ingots in a chest.

"You laugh and answer, 'We are young;
　　O leave us now, and let us grow.'—
Not asking how much more of this
　　Will Time endure or Fate bestow.

"Because a few complacent years
　　Have made your peril of your pride,

Think you that you are to go on
　　Forever pampered and untried?

"What lost eclipse of history,
　　What bivouac of the marching stars,
Has given the sign for you to see
　　Millenniums and last great wars?

"What unrecorded overthrow
　　Of all the world has ever known,
Or ever been, has made itself
　　So plain to you, and you alone?

"Your Dollar, Dove and Eagle make
　　A Trinity that even you
Rate higher than you rate yourselves;
　　It pays, it flatters, and it's new.

"And though your very flesh and blood
　　Be what your Eagle eats and drinks,
You'll praise him for the best of birds,
　　Not knowing what the Eagle thinks.

"The power is yours, but not the sight;
    You see not upon what you tread;
You have the ages for your guide,
    But not the wisdom to be led.

"Think you to tread forever down
    The merciless old verities?
And are you never to have eyes
    To see the world for what it is?

"Are you to pay for what you have
    With all you are?"—No other word
We caught, but with a laughing crowd
    Moved on. None heeded, and few heard.

JOHN GORHAM

"Tell me what you're doing over here, John Gorham,
Sighing hard and seeming to be sorry when you're not;
Make me laugh or let me go now, for long faces in the moon-
   light
Are a sign for me to say again a word that you forgot."—

"I'm over here to tell you what the moon already
May have said or maybe shouted ever since a year ago;
I'm over here to tell you what you are, Jane Wayland,
And to make you rather sorry, I should say, for being so."—

"Tell me what you're saying to me now, John Gorham,
Or you'll never see as much of me as ribbons any more;
I'll vanish in as many ways as I have toes and fingers,
And you'll not follow far for one where flocks have been be-
   fore."—

"I'm sorry now you never saw the flocks, Jane Wayland,
But you're the one to make of them as many as you need.
And then about the vanishing. It's I who mean to vanish;
And when I'm here no longer you'll be done with me indeed."—

"That's a way to tell me what I am, John Gorham!
How am I to know myself until I make you smile?
Try to look as if the moon were making faces at you,
And a little more as if you meant to stay a little while."—

"You are what it is that over rose-blown gardens
Make a pretty flutter for a season in the sun;
You are what it is that with a mouse, Jane Wayland,
Catches him and lets him go and eats him up for fun."—

"Sure I never took you for a mouse, John Gorham;
All you say is easy, but so far from being true
That I wish you wouldn't ever be again the one to think so;
For it isn't cats and butterflies that I would be to you."—

"All your little animals are in one picture—
One I've had before me since a year ago to-night;
And the picture where they live will be of you, Jane Wayland,
Till you find a way to kill them or to keep them out of sight."—

"Won't you ever see me as I am, John Gorham,
Leaving out the foolishness and all I never meant?

Somewhere in me there's a woman, if you know the way to find
   her.
Will you like me any better if I prove it and repent?"—

"I doubt if I shall ever have the time, Jane Wayland;
And I dare say all this moonlight lying round us might as well
Fall for nothing on the shards of broken urns that are forgot-
   ten,
As on two that have no longer much of anything to tell."

STAFFORD'S CABIN

Once there was a cabin here, and once there was a man;
And something happened here before my memory began.
Time has made the two of them the fuel of one flame
And all we have of them is now a legend and a name.

All I have to say is what an old man said to me,
And that would seem to be as much as there will ever be
"Fifty years ago it was we found it where it sat."—
And forty years ago it was old Archibald said that.

"An apple tree that's yet alive saw something, I suppose,
Of what it was that happened there, and what no mortal knows.
Some one on the mountain heard far off a master shriek,
And then there was a light that showed the way for men to
    seek.

"We found it in the morning with an iron bar behind,
And there were chains around it; but no search could ever find,
Either in the ashes that were left, or anywhere,
A sign to tell of who or what had been with Stafford there.

"Stafford was a likely man with ideas of his own—
Though I could never like the kind that likes to live alone;
And when you met, you found his eyes were always on your
   shoes,
As if they did the talking when he asked you for the news.

"That's all, my son. Were I to talk for half a hundred years
I'd never clear away from there the cloud that never clears.
We buried what was left of it,—the bar, too, and the chains;
And only for the apple tree there's nothing that remains."

Forty years ago it was I heard the old man say,
"That's all, my son."—And here again I find the place to-day,
Deserted and told only by the tree that knows the most,
And overgrown with golden-rod as if there were no ghost.

HILLCREST

(To Mrs. Edward MacDowell)

No sound of any storm that shakes
Old island walls with older seas
Comes here where now September makes
An island in a sea of trees.

Between the sunlight and the shade
A man may learn till he forgets
The roaring of a world remade,
And all his ruins and regrets;

And if he still remembers here
Poor fights he may have won or lost,—
If he be ridden with the fear
Of what some other fight may cost,—

If, eager to confuse too soon,
What he has known with what may be,
He reads a planet out of tune
For cause of his jarred harmony,—

If here he venture to unroll
His index of adagios,

And he be given to console
Humanity with what he knows,—

He may by contemplation learn
A little more than what he knew,
And even see great oaks return
To acorns out of which they grew.

He may, if he but listen well,
Through twilight and the silence here,
Be told what there are none may tell
To vanity's impatient ear;

And he may never dare again
Say what awaits him, or be sure
What sunlit labyrinth of pain
He may not enter and endure.

Who knows to-day from yesterday
May learn to count no thing too strange:
Love builds of what Time takes away,
Till Death itself is less than Change.

Who sees enough in his duress
May go as far as dreams have gone;

Who sees a little may do less
Than many who are blind have done;

Who sees unchastened here the soul
Triumphant has no other sight
Than has a child who sees the whole
World radiant with his own delight.

Far journeys and hard wandering
Await him in whose crude surmise
Peace, like a mask, hides everything
That is and has been from his eyes;

And all his wisdom is unfound,
Or like a web that error weaves
On airy looms that have a sound
No louder now than falling leaves.

OLD KING COLE

In Tilbury Town did Old King Cole
A wise old age anticipate,
Desiring, with his pipe and bowl,
No Khan's extravagant estate.
No crown annoyed his honest head,
No fiddlers three were called or needed;
For two disastrous heirs instead
Made music more than ever three did.

Bereft of her with whom his life
Was harmony without a flaw,
He took no other for a wife,
Nor sighed for any that he saw;
And if he doubted his two sons,
And heirs, Alexis and Evander,
He might have been as doubtful once
Of Robert Burns and Alexander.

Alexis, in his early youth,
Began to steal—from old and young.
Likewise Evander, and the truth
Was like a bad taste on his tongue.

Born thieves and liars, their affair
Seemed only to be tarred with evil—
The most insufferable pair
Of scamps that ever cheered the devil.

The world went on, their fame went on,
And they went on—from bad to worse;
Till, goaded hot with nothing done,
And each accoutred with a curse,
The friends of Old King Cole, by twos,
And fours, and sevens, and elevens,
Pronounced unalterable views
Of doings that were not of heaven's.

And having learned again whereby
Their baleful zeal had come about,
King Cole met many a wrathful eye
So kindly that its wrath went out—
Or partly out. Say what they would,
He seemed the more to court their candor;
But never told what kind of good
Was in Alexis and Evander.

And Old King Cole, with many a puff
That haloed his urbanity,
Would smoke till he had smoked enough,
And listen most attentively.
He beamed as with an inward light
That had the Lord's assurance in it;
And once a man was there all night,
Expecting something every minute.

But whether from too little thought,
Or too much fealty to the bowl,
A dim reward was all he got
For sitting up with Old King Cole.
"Though mine," the father mused aloud,
"Are not the sons I would have chosen,
Shall I, less evilly endowed,
By their infirmity be frozen?

"They'll have a bad end, I'll agree,
But I was never born to groan;
For I can see what I can see,
And I'm accordingly alone.
With open heart and open door,

I love my friends, I like my neighbors;
But if I try to tell you more,
Your doubts will overmatch my labors.

"This pipe would never make me calm,
This bowl my grief would never drown.
For grief like mine there is no balm
In Gilead, or in Tilbury Town.
And if I see what I can see,
I know not any way to blind it;
Nor more if any way may be
For you to grope or fly to find it.

"There may be room for ruin yet,
And ashes for a wasted love;
Or, like One whom you may forget,
I may have meat you know not of.
And if I'd rather live than weep
Meanwhile, do you find that surprising?
Why, bless my soul, the man's asleep!
That's good.   The sun will soon be rising."

BEN JONSON ENTERTAINS A MAN FROM STRATFORD

You are a friend then, as I make it out,
Of our man Shakespeare, who alone of us
Will put an ass's head in Fairyland
As he would add a shilling to more shillings,
All most harmonious,—and out of his
Miraculous inviolable increase
Fills Ilion, Rome, or any town you like
Of olden time with timeless Englishmen;
And I must wonder what you think of him—
All you down there where your small Avon flows
By Stratford, and where you're an Alderman.
Some, for a guess, would have him riding back
To be a farrier there, or say a dyer;
Or maybe one of your adept surveyors;
Or like enough the wizard of all tanners.
Not you—no fear of that; for I discern
In you a kindling of the flame that saves—
The nimble element, the true caloric;
I see it, and was told of it, moreover,
By our discriminate friend himself, no other.
Had you been one of the sad average,

As he would have it,—meaning, as I take it,
The sinew and the solvent of our Island,
You'd not be buying beer for this Terpander's
Approved and estimated friend Ben Jonson;
He'd never foist it as a part of his
Contingent entertainment of a townsman
While he goes off rehearsing, as he must,
If he shall ever be the Duke of Stratford.
And my words are no shadow on your town—
Far from it; for one town's as like another
As all are unlike London. Oh, he knows it,—
And there's the Stratford in him; he denies it,
And there's the Shakespeare in him. So, God help him!
I tell him he needs Greek; but neither God
Nor Greek will help him. Nothing will help that man.
You see the fates have given him so much,
He must have all or perish,—or look out
Of London, where he sees too many lords.
They're part of half what ails him: I suppose
There's nothing fouler down among the demons
Than what it is he feels when he remembers
The dust and sweat and ointment of his calling
With his lords looking on and laughing at him.

King as he is, he can't be king *de facto*,
And that's as well, because he wouldn't like it;
He'd frame a lower rating of men then
Than he has now; and after that would come
An abdication or an apoplexy.
He can't be king, not even king of Stratford,—
Though half the world, if not the whole of it,
May crown him with a crown that fits no king
Save Lord Apollo's homesick emissary;
Not there on Avon, or on any stream
Where Naiads and their white arms are no more,
Shall he find home again. It's all too bad.
But there's a comfort, for he'll have that House—
The best you ever saw; and he'll be there
Anon, as you're an Alderman. Good God!
He makes me lie awake o'nights and laugh.

And you have known him from his origin,
You tell me; and a most uncommon urchin
He must have been to the few seeing ones—
A trifle terrifying, I dare say,
Discovering a world with his man's eyes,
Quite as another lad might see some finches,

If he looked hard and had an eye for nature.
But this one had his eyes and their foretelling,
And he had you to fare with, and what else?
He must have had a father and a mother—
In fact I've heard him say so—and a dog,
As a boy should, I venture; and the dog,
Most likely, was the only man who knew him.
A dog, for all I know, is what he needs
As much as anything right here to-day,
To counsel him about his disillusions,
Old aches, and parturitions of what's coming,—
A dog of orders, an emeritus,
To wag his tail at him when he comes home,
And then to put his paws up on his knees
And say, "For God's sake, what's it all about?"

I don't know whether he needs a dog or not—
Or what he needs. I tell him he needs Greek;
I'll talk of rules and Aristotle with him,
And if his tongue's at home he'll say to that,
"I have your word that Aristotle knows,
And you mine that I don't know Aristotle."
He's all at odds with all the unities,

And what's yet worse, it doesn't seem to matter;
He treads along through Time's old wilderness
As if the tramp of all the centuries
Had left no roads—and there are none, for him;
He doesn't see them, even with those eyes,—
And that's a pity, or I say it is.
Accordingly we have him as we have him—
Going his way, the way that he goes best,
A pleasant animal with no great noise
Or nonsense anywhere to set him off—
Save only divers and inclement devils
Have made of late his heart their dwelling place.
A flame half ready to fly out sometimes
At some annoyance may be fanned up in him,
But soon it falls, and when it falls goes out;
He knows how little room there is in there
For crude and futile animosities,
And how much for the joy of being whole,
And how much for long sorrow and old pain.
On our side there are some who may be given
To grow old wondering what he thinks of us
And some above us, who are, in his eyes,
Above himself,—and that's quite right and English.

Yet here we smile, or disappoint the gods
Who made it so: the gods have always eyes
To see men scratch; and they see one down here
Who itches, manor-bitten to the bone,
Albeit he knows himself—yes, yes, he knows—
The lord of more than England and of more
Than all the seas of England in all time
Shall ever wash.   D'ye wonder that I laugh?
He sees me, and he doesn't seem to care;
And why the devil should he?   I can't tell you.

I'll meet him out alone of a bright Sunday,
Trim, rather spruce, and quite the gentleman.
"What ho, my lord!" say I.   He doesn't hear me;
Wherefore I have to pause and look at him.
He's not enormous, but one looks at him.
A little on the round if you insist,
For now, God save the mark, he's growing old;
He's five and forty, and to hear him talk
These days you'd call him eighty; then you'd add
More years to that.   He's old enough to be
The father of a world, and so he is.
"Ben, you're a scholar, what's the time of day?"

Says he; and there shines out of him again
An aged light that has no age or station—
The mystery that's his—a mischievous
Half-mad serenity that laughs at fame
For being won so easy, and at friends
Who laugh at him for what he wants the most,
And for his dukedom down in Warwickshire;—
By which you see we're all a little jealous. . . .
Poor Greene! I fear the color of his name
Was even as that of his ascending soul;
And he was one where there are many others,—
Some scrivening to the end against their fate,
Their puppets all in ink and all to die there;
And some with hands that once would shade an eye
That scanned Euripides and Æschylus
Will reach by this time for a pot-house mop
To slush their first and last of royalties.
Poor devils! and they all play to his hand;
For so it was in Athens and old Rome.
But that's not here or there; I've wandered off.
Greene does it, or I'm careful. Where's that boy?

Yes, he'll go back to Stratford. And we'll miss him?
Dear sir, there'll be no London here without him.

We'll all be riding, one of these fine days,

Down there to see him—and his wife won't like us;

And then we'll think of what he never said

Of women—which, if taken all in all

With what he did say, would buy many horses.

Though nowadays he's not so much for women:

"So few of them," he says, "are worth the guessing."

But there's a worm at work when he says that,

And while he says it one feels in the air

A deal of circumambient hocus-pocus.

They've had him dancing till his toes were tender,

And he can feel 'em now, come chilly rains.

There's no long cry for going into it,

However, and we don't know much about it.

But you in Stratford, like most here in London,

Have more now in the *Sonnets* than you paid for;

He's put one there with all her poison on,

To make a singing fiction of a shadow

That's in his life a fact, and always will be.

But she's no care of ours, though Time, I fear,

Will have a more reverberant ado

About her than about another one

Who seems to have decoyed him, married him,

And sent him scuttling on his way to London,—
With much already learned, and more to learn,
And more to follow. Lord! how I see him now,
Pretending, maybe trying, to be like us.
Whatever he may have meant, we never had him;
He failed us, or escaped, or what you will,—
And there was that about him (God knows what,—
We'd flayed another had he tried it on us)
That made as many of us as had wits
More fond of all his easy distances
Than one another's noise and clap-your-shoulder.
But think you not, my friend, he'd never talk!
Talk? He was eldritch at it; and we listened—
Thereby acquiring much we knew before
About ourselves, and hitherto had held
Irrelevant, or not prime to the purpose.
And there were some, of course, and there be now,
Disordered and reduced amazedly
To resignation by the mystic seal
Of young finality the gods had laid
On everything that made him a young demon;
And one or two shot looks at him already
As he had been their executioner;

And once or twice he was, not knowing it,—
Or knowing, being sorry for poor clay
And saying nothing. . . . Yet, for all his engines,
You'll meet a thousand of an afternoon
Who strut and sun themselves and see around 'em
A world made out of more that has a reason
Than his, I swear, that he sees here to-day;
Though he may scarcely give a Fool an exit
But we mark how he sees in everything
A law that, given we flout it once too often,
Brings fire and iron down on our naked heads.
To me it looks as if the power that made him,
For fear of giving all things to one creature,
Left out the first,—faith, innocence, illusion,
Whatever 'tis that keeps us out o' Bedlam,—
And thereby, for his too consuming vision,
Empowered him out of nature; though to see him,
You'd never guess what's going on inside him.
He'll break out some day like a keg of ale
With too much independent frenzy in it;
And all for cellaring what he knows won't keep,
And what he'd best forget—but that he can't.
You'll have it, and have more than I'm foretelling;

And there'll be such a roaring at the Globe
As never stunned the bleeding gladiators,
He'll have to change the color of its hair
A bit, for now he calls it Cleopatra.
Black hair would never do for Cleopatra.
But you and I are not yet two old women,
And you're a man of office. What he does
Is more to you than how it is he does it,—
And that's what the Lord God has never told him.
They work together, and the Devil helps 'em;
They do it of a morning, or if not,
They do it of a night; in which event
He's peevish of a morning. He seems old;
He's not the proper stomach or the sleep—
And they're two sovran agents to conserve him
Against the fiery art that has no mercy
But what's in that prodigious grand new House.
I gather something happening in his boyhood
Fulfilled him with a boy's determination
To make all Stratford 'ware of him. Well, well,
I hope at last he'll have his joy of it,
And all his pigs and sheep and bellowing beeves,
And frogs and owls and unicorns, moreover,

Be less than hell to his attendant ears.
Oh, past a doubt we'll all go down to see him.

He may be wise.   With London two days off,
Down there some wind of heaven may yet revive him;
But there's no quickening breath from anywhere
Shall make of him again the poised young faun
From Warwickshire, who'd made, it seems, already
A legend of himself before I came
To blink before the last of his first lightning.
Whatever there be, there'll be no more of that;
The coming on of his old monster Time
Has made him a still man; and he has dreams
Were fair to think on once, and all found hollow.
He knows how much of what men paint themselves
Would blister in the light of what they are;
He sees how much of what was great now shares
An eminence transformed and ordinary;
He knows too much of what the world has hushed
In others, to be loud now for himself;
He knows now at what height low enemies
May reach his heart, and high friends let him fall;
But what not even such as he may know

Bedevils him the worst: his lark may sing
At heaven's gate how he will, and for as long
As joy may listen, but *he* sees no gate,
Save one whereat the spent clay waits a little
Before the churchyard has it, and the worm.
Not long ago, late in an afternoon,
I came on him unseen down Lambeth way,
And on my life I was afear'd of him:
He gloomed and mumbled like a soul from Tophet,
His hands behind him and his head bent solemn.
"What is it now," said I,—"another woman?"
That made him sorry for me, and he smiled.
"No, Ben," he mused; "it's Nothing.   It's all Nothing.
We come, we go; and when we're done, we're done.
Spiders and flies—we're mostly one or t'other—
We come, we go; and when we're done, we're done."—
"By God, you sing that song as if you knew it!"
Said I, by way of cheering him; "what ails ye?"
"I think I must have come down here to think,"
Says he to that, and pulls his little beard;
"Your fly will serve as well as anybody,
And what's his hour?   He flies, and flies, and flies,
And in his fly's mind has a brave appearance;

And then your spider gets him in her net,
And eats him out, and hangs him up to dry.
That's Nature, the kind mother of us all.
And then your slattern housemaid swings her broom,
And where's your spider? And that's Nature, also.
It's Nature, and it's Nothing. It's all Nothing.
It's all a world where bugs and emperors
Go singularly back to the same dust,
Each in his time; and the old, ordered stars
That sang together, Ben, will sing the same
Old stave to-morrow."

When he talks like that,
There's nothing for a human man to do
But lead him to some grateful nook like this
Where we be now, and there to make him drink.
He'll drink, for love of me, and then be sick;
A sad sign always in a man of parts,
And always very ominous. The great
Should be as large in liquor as in love,—
And our great friend is not so large in either:
One disaffects him, and the other fails him;
Whatso he drinks that has an antic in it,

He's wondering what's to pay in his insides;
And while his eyes are on the Cyprian
He's fribbling all the time with that damned House.
We laugh here at his thrift, but after all
It may be thrift that saves him from the devil;
God gave it, anyhow,—and we'll suppose
He knew the compound of his handiwork.
To-day the clouds are with him, but anon
He'll out of 'em enough to shake the tree
Of life itself and bring down fruit unheard-of,—
And, throwing in the bruised and whole together,
Prepare a wine to make us drunk with wonder;
And if he live, there'll be a sunset spell
Thrown over him as over a glassed lake
That yesterday was all a black wild water.

God send he live to give us, if no more,
What now's a-rampage in him, and exhibit,
With a decent half-allegiance to the ages
An earnest of at least a casual eye
Turned once on what he owes to Gutenberg,
And to the fealty of more centuries
Than are as yet a picture in our vision.

"There's time enough,—I'll do it when I'm old,
And we're immortal men," he says to that;
And then he says to me, "Ben, what's 'immortal'?
Think you by any force of ordination
It may be nothing of a sort more noisy
Than a small oblivion of component ashes
That of a dream-addicted world was once
A moving atomy much like your friend here?"
Nothing will help that man. To make him laugh,
I said then he was a mad mountebank,—
And by the Lord I nearer made him cry.
I could have eat an eft then, on my knees,
Tail, claws, and all of him; for I had stung
The king of men, who had no sting for me,
And I had hurt him in his memories;
And I say now, as I shall say again,
I love the man this side idolatry.

He'll do it when he's old, he says. I wonder.
He may not be so ancient as all that.
For such as he, the thing that is to do
Will do itself,—but there's a reckoning;
The sessions that are now too much his own,

The roiling inward of a stilled outside,

The churning out of all those blood-fed lines,

The nights of many schemes and little sleep,

The full brain hammered hot with too much thinking,

The vexed heart over-worn with too much aching,—

This weary jangling of conjoined affairs

Made out of elements that have no end,

And all confused at once, I understand,

Is not what makes a man to live forever.

O no, not now! He'll not be going now:

There'll be time yet for God knows what explosions

Before he goes. He'll stay awhile. Just wait:

Just wait a year or two for Cleopatra,

For she's to be a balsam and a comfort;

And that's not all a jape of mine now, either.

For granted once the old way of Apollo

Sings in a man, he may then, if he's able,

Strike unafraid whatever strings he will

Upon the last and wildest of new lyres;

Nor out of his new magic, though it hymn

The shrieks of dungeoned hell, shall he create

A madness or a gloom to shut quite out

A cleaving daylight, and a last great calm

[45]

Triumphant over shipwreck and all storms.
He might have given Aristotle creeps,
But surely would have given him his *katharsis*.

He'll not be going yet. There's too much yet
Unsung within the man. But when he goes,
I'd stake ye coin o' the realm his only care
For a phantom world he sounded and found wanting
Will be a portion here, a portion there,
Of this or that thing or some other thing
That has a patent and intrinsical
Equivalence in those egregious shillings.
And yet he knows, God help him! Tell me, now,
If ever there was anything let loose
On earth by gods or devils heretofore
Like this mad, careful, proud, indifferent Shakespeare!
Where was it, if it ever was? By heaven,
'Twas never yet in Rhodes or Pergamon—
In Thebes or Nineveh, a thing like this!
No thing like this was ever out of England;
And that he knows. I wonder if he cares.
Perhaps he does. . . . O Lord, that House in Stratford!

EROS TURANNOS

She fears him, and will always ask
What fated her to choose him;
She meets in his engaging mask
All reasons to refuse him;
But what she meets and what she fears
Are less than are the downward years,
Drawn slowly to the foamless weirs
Of age, were she to lose him.

Between a blurred sagacity
That once had power to sound him,
And Love, that will not let him be
The Judas that she found him,
Her pride assuages her almost,
As if it were alone the cost.—
He sees that he will not be lost,
And waits and looks around him.

A sense of ocean and old trees
Envelops and allures him;
Tradition, touching all he sees,
Beguiles and reassures him;

And all her doubts of what he says
Are dimmed with what she knows of days—
Till even prejudice delays
    And fades, and she secures him.

The falling leaf inaugurates
    The reign of her confusion;
The pounding wave reverberates
    The dirge of her illusion;
And home, where passion lived and died,
Becomes a place where she can hide,
While all the town and harbor side
    Vibrate with her seclusion.

We tell you, tapping on our brows,
    The story as it should be,—
As if the story of a house
    Were told, or ever could be;
We'll have no kindly veil between
Her visions and those we have seen,—
As if we guessed what hers have been,
    Or what they are or would be.

Meanwhile we do no harm; for they
     That with a god have striven,
Not hearing much of what we say,
     Take what the god has given;
Though like waves breaking it may be,
Or like a changed familiar tree,
Or like a stairway to the sea
     Where down the blind are driven.

OLD TRAILS

(Washington Square)

I met him, as one meets a ghost or two,
Between the gray Arch and the old Hotel.
"King Solomon was right, there's nothing new,"
Said he. "Behold a ruin who meant well."

He led me down familiar steps again,
Appealingly, and set me in a chair.
"My dreams have all come true, to other men,"
Said he; "God lives, however, and why care?

"An hour among the ghosts will do no harm."
He laughed, and something glad within me sank.
I may have eyed him with a faint alarm,
For now his laugh was lost in what he drank.

"They chill things here with ice from hell," he said;
"I might have known it." And he made a face
That showed again how much of him was dead,
And how much was alive and out of place,

And out of reach. He knew as well as I
That all the words of wise men who are skilled
In using them are not much to defy
What comes when memory meets the unfulfilled.

What evil and infirm perversity
Had been at work with him to bring him back?
Never among the ghosts, assuredly,
Would he originate a new attack;

Never among the ghosts, or anywhere,
Till what was dead of him was put away,
Would he attain to his offended share
Of honor among others of his day.

"You ponder like an owl," he said at last;
"You always did, and here you have a cause.
For I'm a confirmation of the past,
A vengeance, and a flowering of what was.

"Sorry? Of course you are, though you compress,
With even your most impenetrable fears,
A placid and a proper consciousness
Of anxious angels over my arrears.

"I see them there against me in a book
As large as hope, in ink that shines by night.
Surely I see; but now I'd rather look
At you, and you are not a pleasant sight.

"Forbear, forgive. Ten years are on my soul,
And on my conscience. I've an incubus:
My one distinction, and a parlous toll
To glory; but hope lives on clamorous.

" 'Twas hope, though heaven I grant you knows of what—
The kind that blinks and rises when it falls,
Whether it sees a reason why or not—
That heard Broadway's hard-throated siren-calls;

" 'Twas hope that brought me through December storms,
To shores again where I'll not have to be
A lonely man with only foreign worms
To cheer him in his last obscurity.

"But what it was that hurried me down here
To be among the ghosts, I leave to you.
My thanks are yours, no less, for one thing clear:
Though you are silent, what you say is true.

"There may have been the devil in my feet,
For down I blundered, like a fugitive,
To find the old room in Eleventh Street.
God save us!—I came here again to live."

We rose at that, and all the ghosts rose then,
And followed us unseen to his old room.
No longer a good place for living men
We found it, and we shivered in the gloom.

The goods he took away from there were few,
And soon we found ourselves outside once more,
Where now the lamps along the Avenue
Bloomed white for miles above an iron floor.

"Now lead me to the newest of hotels,"
He said, "and let your spleen be undeceived:
This ruin is not myself, but some one else;
I haven't failed; I've merely not achieved."

Whether he knew or not, he laughed and dined
With more of an immune regardlessness
Of pits before him and of sands behind
Than many a child at forty would confess;

And after, when the bells in *Boris* rang
Their tumult at the Metropolitan,
He rocked himself, and I believe he sang.
"God lives," he crooned aloud, "and I'm the man!"

He was.   And even though the creature spoiled
All prophecies, I cherish his acclaim.
Three weeks he fattened; and five years he toiled
In Yonkers,—and then sauntered into fame.

And he may go now to what streets he will—
Eleventh, or the last, and little care;
But he would find the old room very still
Of evenings, and the ghosts would all be there.

I doubt if he goes after them; I doubt
If many of them ever come to him.
His memories are like lamps, and they go out;
Or if they burn, they flicker and are dim.

A light of other gleams he has to-day
And adulations of applauding hosts;

A famous danger, but a safer way
Than growing old alone among the ghosts.

But we may still be glad that we were wrong:
He fooled us, and we'd shrivel to deny it;
Though sometimes when old echoes ring too long,
I wish the bells in *Boris* would be quiet.

THE UNFORGIVEN

When he, who is the unforgiven,
Beheld her first, he found her fair:
No promise ever dreamt in heaven
Could then have lured him anywhere
That would have been away from there;
And all his wits had lightly striven,
Foiled with her voice, and eyes, and hair.

There's nothing in the saints and sages
To meet the shafts her glances had,
Or such as hers have had for ages
To blind a man till he be glad,
And humble him till he be mad.
The story would have many pages,
And would be neither good nor bad.

And, having followed, you would find him
Where properly the play begins;
But look for no red light behind him—
No fumes of many-colored sins,
Fanned high by screaming violins.

God knows what good it was to blind him,
Or whether man or woman wins.

And by the same eternal token,
Who knows just how it will all end?—
This drama of hard words unspoken,
This fireside farce, without a friend
Or enemy to comprehend
What augurs when two lives are broken,
And fear finds nothing left to mend.

He stares in vain for what awaits him,
And sees in Love a coin to toss;
He smiles, and her cold hush berates him
Beneath his hard half of the cross;
They wonder why it ever was;
And she, the unforgiving, hates him
More for her lack than for her loss.

He feeds with pride his indecision,
And shrinks from what will not occur,
Bequeathing with infirm derision
His ashes to the days that were,

Before she made him prisoner;
And labors to retrieve the vision
That he must once have had of her.

He waits, and there awaits an ending,
And he knows neither what nor when;
But no magicians are attending
To make him see as he saw then,
And he will never find again
The face that once had been the rending
Of all his purpose among men.

He blames her not, nor does he chide her,
And she has nothing new to say;
If he were Bluebeard he could hide her,
But that's not written in the play,
And there will be no change to-day;
Although, to the serene outsider,
There still would seem to be a way.

THEOPHILUS

By what serene malevolence of names
Had you the gift of yours, Theophilus?
Not even a smeared young Cyclops at his games
Would have you long,—and you are one of us.

Told of your deeds I shudder for your dreams
And they, no doubt, are few and innocent.
Meanwhile, I marvel; for in you, it seems,
Heredity outshines environment.

What lingering bit of Belial, unforeseen,
Survives and amplifies itself in you?
What manner of devilry has ever been
That your obliquity may never do?

Humility befits a father's eyes,
But not a friend of us would have him weep.
Admiring everything that lives and dies,
Theophilus, we like you best asleep.

Sleep—sleep; and let us find another man
To lend another name less hazardous:
Caligula, maybe, or Caliban,
Or Cain,—but surely not Theophilus.

VETERAN SIRENS

The ghost of Ninon would be sorry now
To laugh at them, were she to see them here,
So brave and so alert for learning how
To fence with reason for another year.

Age offers a far comelier diadem
Than theirs; but anguish has no eye for grace,
When time's malicious mercy cautions them
To think a while of number and of space.

The burning hope, the worn expectancy,
The martyred humor, and the maimed allure,
Cry out for time to end his levity,
And age to soften its investiture;

But they, though others fade and are still fair,
Defy their fairness and are unsubdued;
Although they suffer, they may not forswear
The patient ardor of the unpursued.

Poor flesh, to fight the calendar so long;
Poor vanity, so quaint and yet so brave;
Poor folly, so deceived and yet so strong,
So far from Ninon and so near the grave.

SIEGE PERILOUS

Long warned of many terrors more severe
To scorch him than hell's engines could awaken,
He scanned again, too far to be so near,
The fearful seat no man had ever taken.

So many other men with older eyes
Than his to see with older sight behind them
Had known so long their one way to be wise,—
Was any other thing to do than mind them?

So many a blasting parallel had seared
Confusion on his faith,—could he but wonder
If he were mad and right, or if he feared
God's fury told in shafted flame and thunder?

There fell one day upon his eyes a light
Ethereal, and he heard no more men speaking;
He saw their shaken heads, but no long sight
Was his but for the end that he went seeking.

The end he sought was not the end; the crown
He won shall unto many still be given.
Moreover, there was reason here to frown:
No fury thundered, no flame fell from heaven.

ANOTHER DARK LADY

Think not, because I wonder where you fled,
That I would lift a pin to see you there;
You may, for me, be prowling anywhere,
So long as you show not your little head:
No dark and evil story of the dead
Would leave you less pernicious or less fair—
Not even Lilith, with her famous hair;
And Lilith was the devil, I have read.

I cannot hate you, for I loved you then.
The woods were golden then.   There was a road
Through beeches; and I said their smooth feet showed
Like yours.   Truth must have heard me from afar,
For I shall never have to learn again
That yours are cloven as no beech's are.

THE VOICE OF AGE

She'd look upon us, if she could,
As hard as Rhadamanthus would;
Yet one may see,—who sees her face,
Her crown of silver and of lace,
Her mystical serene address
Of age alloyed with loveliness,—
That she would not annihilate
The frailest of things animate.

She has opinions of our ways,
And if we're not all mad, she says,—
If our ways are not wholly worse
Than others, for not being hers,—
There might somehow be found a few
Less insane things for us to do,
And we might have a little heed
Of what Belshazzar couldn't read.

She feels, with all our furniture,
Room yet for something more secure
Than our self-kindled aureoles
To guide our poor forgotten souls;

But when we have explained that grace
Dwells now in doing for the race,
She nods—as if she were relieved;
Almost as if she were deceived.

She frowns at much of what she hears,
And shakes her head, and has her fears;
Though none may know, by any chance,
What rose-leaf ashes of romance
Are faintly stirred by later days
That would be well enough, she says,
If only people were more wise,
And grown-up children used their eyes.

THE DARK HOUSE

Where a faint light shines alone,
Dwells a Demon I have known.
Most of you had better say
"The Dark House," and go your way.
Do not wonder if I stay.

For I know the Demon's eyes,
And their lure that never dies.
Banish all your fond alarms,
For I know the foiling charms
Of her eyes and of her arms.

And I know that in one room
Burns a lamp as in a tomb;
And I see the shadow glide,
Back and forth, of one denied
Power to find himself outside.

There he is who is my friend,
Damned, he fancies, to the end—
Vanquished, ever since a door

Closed, he thought, for evermore
On the life that was before.

And the friend who knows him best
Sees him as he sees the rest
Who are striving to be wise
While a Demon's arms and eyes
Hold them as a web would flies.

All the words of all the world,
Aimed together and then hurled,
Would be stiller in his ears
Than a closing of still shears
On a thread made out of years.

But there lives another sound,
More compelling, more profound;
There's a music, so it seems,
That assuages and redeems,
More than reason, more than dreams.

There's a music yet unheard
By the creature of the word,

Though it matters little more
Than a wave-wash on a shore—
Till a Demon shuts a door.

So, if he be very still
With his Demon, and one will,
Murmurs of it may be blown
To my friend who is alone
In a room that I have known.

After that from everywhere
Singing life will find him there;
Then the door will open wide,
And my friend, again outside,
Will be living, having died.

THE POOR RELATION

No longer torn by what she knows
And sees within the eyes of others,
Her doubts are when the daylight goes,
Her fears are for the few she bothers.
She tells them it is wholly wrong
Of her to stay alive so long;
And when she smiles her forehead shows
A crinkle that had been her mother's.

Beneath her beauty, blanched with pain,
And wistful yet for being cheated,
A child would seem to ask again
A question many times repeated;
But no rebellion has betrayed
Her wonder at what she has paid
For memories that have no stain,
For triumph born to be defeated.

To those who come for what she was—
The few left who know where to find her—
She clings, for they are all she has;
And she may smile when they remind her,

As heretofore, of what they know
Of roses that are still to blow
By ways where not so much as grass
Remains of what she sees behind her.

They stay a while, and having done
What penance or the past requires,
They go, and leave her there alone
To count her chimneys and her spires.
Her lip shakes when they go away,
And yet she would not have them stay;
She knows as well as anyone
That Pity, having played, soon tires.

But one friend always reappears,
A good ghost, not to be forsaken;
Whereat she laughs and has no fears
Of what a ghost may reawaken,
But welcomes, while she wears and mends
The poor relation's odds and ends,
Her truant from a tomb of years—
Her power of youth so early taken.

Poor laugh, more slender than her song
It seems; and there are none to hear it
With even the stopped ears of the strong
For breaking heart or broken spirit.
The friends who clamored for her place,
And would have scratched her for her face,
Have lost her laughter for so long
That none would care enough to fear it.

None live who need fear anything
From her, whose losses are their pleasure;
The plover with a wounded wing
Stays not the flight that others measure;
So there she waits, and while she lives,
And death forgets, and faith forgives,
Her memories go foraging
For bits of childhood song they treasure.

And like a giant harp that hums
On always, and is always blending
The coming of what never comes
With what has past and had an ending,
The City trembles, throbs, and pounds

Outside, and through a thousand sounds
The small intolerable drums
Of Time are like slow drops descending.

Bereft enough to shame a sage
And given little to long sighing,
With no illusion to assuage
The lonely changelessness of dying,—
Unsought, unthought-of, and unheard,
She sings and watches like a bird,
Safe in a comfortable cage
From which there will be no more flying.

THE BURNING BOOK

Or the Contented Metaphysician

To the lore of no manner of men
  Would his vision have yielded
When he found what will never again
  From his vision be shielded,—
Though he paid with as much of his life
  As a nun could have given,
And to-night would have been as a knife,
  Devil-drawn, devil-driven.

For to-night, with his flame-weary eyes
  On the work he is doing,
He considers the tinder that flies
  And the quick flame pursuing.
In the leaves that are crinkled and curled
  Are his ashes of glory,
And what once were an end of the world
  Is an end of a story.

But he smiles, for no more shall his days
  Be a toil and a calling

For a way to make others to gaze
  On God's face without falling.
He has come to the end of his words,
  And alone he rejoices
In the choiring that silence affords
  Of ineffable voices.

To a realm that his words may not reach
  He may lead none to find him;
An adept, and with nothing to teach,
  He leaves nothing behind him.
For the rest, he will have his release,
  And his embers, attended
By the large and unclamoring peace
  Of a dream that is ended.

FRAGMENT

Faint white pillars that seem to fade
As you look from here are the first one sees
Of his house where it hides and dies in a shade
Of beeches and oaks and hickory trees.
Now many a man, given woods like these,
And a house like that, and the Briony gold,
Would have said, "There are still some gods to please,
And houses are built without hands, we're told."

There are the pillars, and all gone gray.
Briony's hair went white. You may see
Where the garden was if you come this way.
That sun-dial scared him, he said to me;
"Sooner or later they strike," said he,
And he never got that from the books he read.
Others are flourishing, worse than he,
But he knew too much for the life he led.

And who knows all knows everything
That a patient ghost at last retrieves;
There's more to be known of his harvesting

When Time the thresher unbinds the sheaves;
And there's more to be heard than a wind that grieves
For Briony now in this ageless oak,
Driving the first of its withered leaves
Over the stones where the fountain broke.

LISETTE AND EILEEN

"When he was here alive, Eileen,
There was a word you might have said;
So never mind what I have been,
Or anything,—for you are dead.

"And after this when I am there
Where he is, you'll be dying still.
Your eyes are dead, and your black hair,—
The rest of you be what it will.

"'Twas all to save him? Never mind,
Eileen. You saved him. You are strong.
I'd hardly wonder if your kind
Paid everything, for you live long.

"You last, I mean. That's what I mean.
I mean you last as long as lies.
You might have said that word, Eileen,—
And you might have your hair and eyes.

"And what you see might be Lisette,
Instead of this that has no name.

Your silence—I can feel it yet,
Alive and in me, like a flame.

"Where might I be with him to-day,
Could he have known before he heard?
But no—your silence had its way,
Without a weapon or a word.

"Because a word was never told,
I'm going as a worn toy goes.
And you are dead; and you'll be old;
And I forgive you, I suppose.

"I'll soon be changing as all do,
To something we have always been;
And you'll be old. . . . He liked you, too,
I might have killed you then, Eileen.

"I think he liked as much of you
As had a reason to be seen,—
As much as God made black and blue.
He liked your hair and eyes, Eileen."

LLEWELLYN AND THE TREE

Could he have made Priscilla share
  The paradise that he had planned,
Llewellyn would have loved his wife
  As well as any in the land.

Could he have made Priscilla cease
  To goad him for what God left out,
Llewellyn would have been as mild
  As any we have read about.

Could all have been as all was not,
  Llewellyn would have had no story;
He would have stayed a quiet man
  And gone his quiet way to glory.

But howsoever mild he was
  Priscilla was implacable;
And whatsoever timid hopes
  He built—she found them, and they fell.

And this went on, with intervals
  Of labored harmony between

Resounding discords, till at last
   Llewellyn turned—as will be seen.

Priscilla, warmer than her name,
   And shriller than the sound of saws,
Pursued Llewellyn once too far,
   Not knowing quite the man he was.

The more she said, the fiercer clung
   The stinging garment of his wrath;
And this was all before the day
   When Time tossed roses in his path.

Before the roses ever came
   Llewellyn had already risen.
The roses may have ruined him,
   They may have kept him out of prison.

And she who brought them, being Fate,
   Made roses do the work of spears,—
Though many made no more of her
   Than civet, coral, rouge, and years.

You ask us what Llewellyn saw,
    But why ask what may not be given?
To some will come a time when change
    Itself is beauty, if not heaven.

One afternoon Priscilla spoke,
    And her shrill history was done;
At any rate, she never spoke
    Like that again to anyone.

One gold October afternoon
    Great fury smote the silent air;
And then Llewellyn leapt and fled
    Like one with hornets in his hair.

Llewellyn left us, and he said
    Forever, leaving few to doubt him;
And so, through frost and clicking leaves,
    The Tilbury way went on without him.

And slowly, through the Tilbury mist,
    The stillness of October gold
Went out like beauty from a face.
    Priscilla watched it, and grew old.

He fled, still clutching in his flight
     The roses that had been his fall;
The Scarlet One, as you surmise,
     Fled with him, coral, rouge, and all.

Priscilla, waiting, saw the change
     Of twenty slow October moons;
And then she vanished, in her turn
     To be forgotten, like old tunes.

So they were gone—all three of them,
     I should have said, and said no more,
Had not a face once on Broadway
     Been one that I had seen before.

The face and hands and hair were old,
     But neither time nor penury
Could quench within Llewellyn's eyes
     The shine of his one victory.

The roses, faded and gone by,
     Left ruin where they once had reigned;
But on the wreck, as on old shells,
     The color of the rose remained.

His fictive merchandise I bought
For him to keep and show again,
Then led him slowly from the crush
Of his cold-shouldered fellow men.

"And so, Llewellyn," I began—
"Not so," he said; "not so at all:
I've tried the world, and found it good,
For more than twenty years this fall.

"And what the world has left of me
Will go now in a little while."
And what the world had left of him
Was partly an unholy guile.

"That I have paid for being calm
Is what you see, if you have eyes;
For let a man be calm too long,
He pays for much before he dies.

"Be calm when you are growing old
And you have nothing else to do;
Pour not the wine of life too thin
If water means the death of you.

"You say I might have learned at home
    The truth in season to be strong?
Not so; I took the wine of life
    Too thin, and I was calm too long.

"Like others who are strong too late,
    For me there was no going back;
For I had found another speed,
    And I was on the other track.

"God knows how far I might have gone
    Or what there might have been to see;
But my speed had a sudden end,
    And here you have the end of me."

The end or not, it may be now
    But little farther from the truth
To say those worn satiric eyes
    Had something of immortal youth.

He may among the millions here
    Be one, or he may, quite as well,
Be gone to find again the Tree
    Of Knowledge, out of which he fell;

He may be near us, dreaming yet
Of unrepented rouge and coral;
Or in a grave without a name
May be as far off as a moral.

BEWICK FINZER

Time was when his half million drew
   The breath of six per cent;
But soon the worm of what-was-not
   Fed hard on his content;
And something crumbled in his brain
   When his half million went.

Time passed, and filled along with his
   The place of many more;
Time came, and hardly one of us
   Had credence to restore,
From what appeared one day, the man
   Whom we had known before.

The broken voice, the withered neck,
   The coat worn out with care,
The cleanliness of indigence,
   The brilliance of despair,
The fond imponderable dreams
   Of affluence,—all were there.

Poor Finzer, with his dreams and schemes,
  Fares hard now in the race,
With heart and eye that have a task
  When he looks in the face
Of one who might so easily
  Have been in Finzer's place.

He comes unfailing for the loan
  We give and then forget;
He comes, and probably for years
  Will he be coming yet,—
Familiar as an old mistake,
  And futile as regret.

BOKARDO

Well, Bokardo, here we are;
  Make yourself at home.
Look around—you haven't far
  To look—and why be dumb?
Not the place that used to be,
Not so many things to see;
But there's room for you and me.
  And you—you've come.

Talk a little; or, if not,
  Show me with a sign
Why it was that you forgot
  What was yours and mine.
Friends, I gather, are small things
In an age when coins are kings;
Even at that, one hardly flings
  Friends before swine.

Rather strong? I knew as much,
  For it made you speak.
No offense to swine, as such,

But why this hide-and-seek?
You have something on your side,
And you wish you might have died,
So you tell me.   And you tried
   One night last week?

You tried hard?   And even then
   Found a time to pause?
When you try as hard again,
   You'll have another cause.
When you find yourself at odds
With all dreamers of all gods,
You may smite yourself with rods—
   But not the laws.

Though they seem to show a spite
   Rather devilish,
They move on as with a might
   Stronger than your wish.
Still, however strong they be,
They bide man's authority:
Xerxes, when he flogged the sea,
   May've scared a fish.

It's a comfort, if you like,
  To keep honor warm,
But as often as you strike
  The laws, you do no harm.
To the laws, I mean. To you—
That's another point of view,
One you may as well indue
  With some alarm.

Not the most heroic face
  To present, I grant;
Nor will you insure disgrace
  By fearing what you want.
Freedom has a world of sides,
And if reason once derides
Courage, then your courage hides
  A deal of cant.

Learn a little to forget
  Life was once a feast;
You aren't fit for dying yet,
  So don't be a beast.
Few men with a mind will say,

Thinking twice, that they can pay
Half their debts of yesterday,
   Or be released.

There's a debt now on your mind
   More than any gold?
And there's nothing you can find
   Out there in the cold?
Only—what's his name?—Remorse?
And Death riding on his horse?
Well, be glad there's nothing worse
   Than you have told.

Leave Remorse to warm his hands
   Outside in the rain.
As for Death, he understands,
   And he will come again.
Therefore, till your wits are clear,
Flourish and be quiet—here.
But a devil at each ear
   Will be a strain?

Past a doubt they will indeed,
   More than you have earned.

I say that because you need
    Ablution, being burned?
Well, if you must have it so,
Your last flight went rather low.
Better say you had to know
    What you have learned.

And that's over.   Here you are,
    Battered by the past.
Time will have his little scar,
    But the wound won't last.
Nor shall harrowing surprise
Find a world without its eyes
If a star fades when the skies
    Are overcast.

God knows there are lives enough.
    Crushed, and too far gone
Longer to make sermons of,
    And those we leave alone.
Others, if they will, may rend
The worn patience of a friend
Who, though smiling, sees the end,
    With nothing done.

But your fervor to be free
    Fled the faith it scorned;
Death demands a decency
    Of you, and you are warned.
But for all we give we get
Mostly blows? Don't be upset;
You, Bokardo, are not yet
    Consumed or mourned.

There'll be falling into view
    Much to rearrange;
And there'll be a time for you
    To marvel at the change.
They that have the least to fear
Question hardest what is here;
When long-hidden skies are clear,
    The stars look strange.

THE MAN AGAINST THE SKY

Between me and the sunset, like a dome
Against the glory of a world on fire,
Now burned a sudden hill,
Bleak, round, and high, by flame-lit height made higher,
With nothing on it for the flame to kill
Save one who moved and was alone up there
To loom before the chaos and the glare
As if he were the last god going home
Unto his last desire.

Dark, marvelous, and inscrutable he moved on
Till down the fiery distance he was gone,
Like one of those eternal, remote things
That range across a man's imaginings
When a sure music fills him and he knows
What he may say thereafter to few men,—
The touch of ages having *performed* wrought
An echo and a glimpse of what he thought
A phantom or a legend until then;
For whether lighted over ways that save,
Or lured from all repose,

If he go on too far to find a grave,
Mostly alone he goes.

Even he, who stood where I had found him,
On high with fire all round him,
Who moved along the molten west,
And over the round hill's crest
That seemed half ready with him to go down,
Flame-bitten and flame-cleft,
As if there were to be no last thing left
Of a nameless unimaginable town,—
Even he who climbed and vanished may have taken
Down to the perils of a depth not known,
From death defended though by men forsaken,
The bread that every man must eat alone;
He may have walked while others hardly dared
Look on to see him stand where many fell;
And upward out of that, as out of hell,
He may have sung and striven
To mount where more of him shall yet be given,
Bereft of all retreat,
To sevenfold heat,—
As on a day when three in Dura shared

The furnace, and were spared
For glory by that king of Babylon
Who made himself so great that God, who heard,
Covered him with long feathers, like a bird.

Again, he may have gone down easily,
By comfortable altitudes, and found,
As always, underneath him solid ground
Whereon to be sufficient and to stand
Possessed already of the promised land,
Far stretched and fair to see:
A good sight, verily,
And one to make the eyes of her who bore him
Shine glad with hidden tears.
Why question of his ease of who before him,
In one place or another where they left
Their names as far behind them as their bones,
And yet by dint of slaughter toil and theft,
And shrewdly sharpened stones,
Carved hard the way for his ascendency
Through deserts of lost years?
Why trouble him now who sees and hears
No more than what his innocence requires,

And therefore to no other height aspires
Than one at which he neither quails nor tires?
He may do more by seeing what he sees
Than others eager for iniquities;
He may, by seeing all things for the best,
Incite futurity to do the rest.

Or with an even likelihood,
He may have met with atrabilious eyes
The fires of time on equal terms and passed
Indifferently down, until at last
His only kind of grandeur would have been,
Apparently, in being seen.
He may have had for evil or for good
No argument; he may have had no care
For what without himself went anywhere
To failure or to glory, and least of all
For such a stale, flamboyant miracle;
He may have been the prophet of an art
Immovable to old idolatries;
He may have been a player without a part,
Annoyed that even the sun should have the skies

For such a flaming way to advertise;
He may have been a painter sick at heart
With Nature's toiling for a new surprise;
He may have been a cynic, who now, for all
Of anything divine that his effete
Negation may have tasted,
Saw truth in his own image, rather small,
Forbore to fever the ephemeral,
Found any barren height a good retreat
From any swarming street,
And in the sun saw power superbly wasted;
And when the primitive old-fashioned stars
Came out again to shine on joys and wars
More primitive, and all arrayed for doom,
He may have proved a world a sorry thing
In his imagining,
And life a lighted highway to the tomb.

Or, mounting with infirm unsearching tread,
His hopes to chaos led,
He may have stumbled up there from the past,
And with an aching strangeness viewed the last

Abysmal conflagration of his dreams,—
A flame where nothing seems
To burn but flame itself, by nothing fed;
And while it all went out,
Not even the faint anodyne of doubt
May then have eased a painful going down
From pictured heights of power and lost renown,
Revealed at length to his outlived endeavor
Remote and unapproachable for ever;
And at his heart there may have gnawed
Sick memories of a dead faith foiled and flawed
And long dishonored by the living death
Assigned alike by chance
To brutes and hierophants;
And anguish fallen on those he loved around him
May once have dealt the last blow to confound him,
And so have left him as death leaves a child,
Who sees it all too near;
And he who knows no young way to forget
May struggle to the tomb unreconciled.
Whatever suns may rise or set
There may be nothing kinder for him here
Than shafts and agonies;

And under these
He may cry out and stay on horribly;
Or, seeing in death too small a thing to fear,
He may go forward like a stoic Roman
Where pangs and terrors in his pathway lie,—
Or, seizing the swift logic of a woman,
Curse God and die.

Or maybe there, like many another one
Who might have stood aloft and looked ahead,
Black-drawn against wild red,
He may have built, unawed by fiery gules
That in him no commotion stirred,
A living reason out of molecules
Why molecules occurred,
And one for smiling when he might have sighed
Had he seen far enough,
And in the same inevitable stuff
Discovered an odd reason too for pride
In being what he must have been by laws
Infrangible and for no kind of cause.
Deterred by no confusion or surprise

He may have seen with his mechanic eyes
A world without a meaning, and had room,
Alone amid magnificence and doom,
To build himself an airy monument
That should, or fail him in his vague intent,
Outlast an accidental universe—
To call it nothing worse—
Or, by the burrowing guile
Of Time disintegrated and effaced,
Like once-remembered mighty trees go down
To ruin, of which by man may now be traced
No part sufficient even to be rotten,
And in the book of things that are forgotten
Is entered as a thing not quite worth while.
He may have been so great
That satraps would have shivered at his frown,
And all he prized alive may rule a state
No larger than a grave that holds a clown;
He may have been a master of his fate,
And of his atoms,—ready as another
In his emergence to exonerate
His father and his mother;
He may have been a captain of a host,

Self-eloquent and ripe for prodigies.
Doomed here to swell by dangerous degrees,
And then give up the ghost.
Nahum's great grasshoppers were such as these,
Sun-scattered and soon lost...

Whatever the dark road he may have taken,
This man who stood on high
And faced alone the sky,
Whatever drove or lured or guided him,—
A vision answering a faith unshaken,
An easy trust assumed of easy trials,
A sick negation born of weak denials,
A crazed abhorrence of an old condition,
A blind attendance on a brief ambition,—
Whatever stayed him or derided him,
His way was even as ours;
And we, with all our wounds and all our powers,
Must each await alone at his own height
Another darkness or another light;
And there, of our poor self-dominion reft,
If inference and reason shun

Hell, Heaven, and Oblivion,
May thwarted will (perforce precarious,
But for our conservation better thus)
Have no misgiving left
Of doing yet what here we leave undone?
Or if unto the last of these we cleave,
Believing or protesting we believe
In such an idle and ephemeral
Florescence of the diabolical,—
If, robbed of two fond old enormities,
Our being had no onward auguries,
What then were this great love of ours to say
For launching other lives to voyage again
A little farther into time and pain,
A little faster in a futile chase
For a kingdom and a power and a Race
That would have still in sight
A manifest end of ashes and eternal night?
Is this the music of the toys we shake
So loud,—as if there might be no mistake
Somewhere in our indomitable will?
Are we no greater than the noise we make
Along one blind atomic pilgrimage

Whereon by crass chance billeted we go
Because our brains and bones and cartilage
Will have it so?
If this we say, then let us all be still
About our share in it, and live and die
More quietly thereby.

Where was he going, this man against the sky?
You know not, nor do I.
But this we know, if we know anything:
That we may laugh and fight and sing
And of our transience here make offering
To an orient Word that will not be erased,
Or, save in incommunicable gleams
Too permanent for dreams,
Be found or known.
No tonic and ambitious irritant
Of increase or of want
Has made an otherwise insensate waste
Of ages overthrown
A ruthless, veiled, implacable foretaste
Of other ages that are still to be

Depleted and rewarded variously

Because a few, by fate's economy,

Shall seem to move the world the way it goes;

No soft evangel of equality,

Safe-cradled in a communal repose

That huddles into death and may at last

Be covered well with equatorial snows—

And all for what, the devil only knows—

Will aggregate an inkling to confirm

The credit of a sage or of a worm,

Or tell us why one man in five

Should have a care to stay alive

While in his heart he feels no violence

Laid on his humor and intelligence

When infant Science makes a pleasant face

And waves again that hollow toy, the Race;

No planetary trap where souls are wrought

For nothing but the sake of being caught

And sent again to nothing will attune

Itself to any key of any reason

Why man should hunger through another season

To find out why 'twere better late than soon

To go away and let the sun and moon

And all the silly stars illuminate
A place for creeping things,
And those that root and trumpet and have wings,
And herd and ruminate,
Or dive and flash and poise in rivers and seas,
Or by their loyal tails in lofty trees
Hang screeching lewd victorious derision
Of man's immortal vision.

Shall we, because Eternity records
Too vast an answer for the time-born words
We spell, whereof so many are dead that once
In our capricious lexicons
Were so alive and final, hear no more
The Word itself, the living word
That none alive has ever heard
Or ever spelt,
And few have ever felt
Without the fears and old surrenderings
And terrors that began
When Death let fall a feather from his wings
And humbled the first man?

Because the weight of our humility,
Wherefrom we gain
A little wisdom and much pain,
Falls here too sore and there too tedious,
Are we in anguish or complacency,
Not looking far enough ahead
To see by what mad couriers we are led
Along the roads of the ridiculous,
To pity ourselves and laugh at faith
And while we curse life bear it?
And if we see the soul's dead end in death,
Are we to fear it?
What folly is here that has not yet a name
Unless we say outright that we are liars?
What have we seen beyond our sunset fires
That lights again the way by which we came?
Why pay we such a price, and one we give
So clamoringly, for each racked empty day
That leads one more last human hope away,
As quiet fiends would lead past our crazed eyes
Our children to an unseen sacrifice?
If after all that we have lived and thought,
All comes to Nought,—

If there be nothing after Now,
And we be nothing anyhow,
And we know that,—why live?
'Twere sure but weaklings' vain distress
To suffer dungeons where so many doors
Will open on the cold eternal shores
That look sheer down
To the dark tideless floods of Nothingness
Where all who know may drown.

THE TOWN DOWN THE RIVER
(1910)

To Theodore Roosevelt

THE MASTER*

(Lincoln)

A flying word from here and there
Had sown the name at which we sneered,
But soon the name was everywhere,
To be reviled and then revered:
A presence to be loved and feared,
We cannot hide it, or deny
That we, the gentlemen who jeered,
May be forgotten by and by.

He came when days were perilous
And hearts of men were sore beguiled;
And having made his note of us,
He pondered and was reconciled
Was ever master yet so mild
As he, and so untamable?
We doubted, even when he smiled,
Not knowing what he knew so well.

* Supposed to have been written not long after the Civil War.

He knew that undeceiving fate
Would shame us whom he served unsought;
He knew that he must wince and wait—
The jest of those for whom he fought;
He knew devoutly what he thought
Of us and of our ridicule;
He knew that we must all be taught
Like little children in a school.

We gave a glamour to the task
That he encountered and saw through,
But little of us did he ask,
And little did we ever do.
And what appears if we review
The season when we railed and chaffed?
It is the face of one who knew
That we were learning while we laughed.

The face that in our vision feels
Again the venom that we flung,
Transfigured to the world reveals
The vigilance to which we clung.

Shrewd, hallowed, harassed, and among
The mysteries that are untold,
The face we see was never young
Nor could it wholly have been old.

For he, to whom we had applied
Our shopman's test of age and worth,
Was elemental when he died,
As he was ancient at his birth:
The saddest among kings of earth,
Bowed with a galling crown, this man
Met rancor with a cryptic mirth,
Laconic—and Olympian.

The love, the grandeur, and the fame
Are bounded by the world alone;
The calm, the smouldering, and the flame
Of awful patience were his own:
With him they are forever flown
Past all our fond self-shadowings,
Wherewith we cumber the Unknown
As with inept, Icarian wings.

[3]

For we were not as other men:
'Twas ours to soar and his to see;
But we are coming down again,
And we shall come down pleasantly;
Nor shall we longer disagree
On what it is to be sublime,
But flourish in our perigee
And have one Titan at a time.

THE TOWN DOWN THE RIVER

I

Said the Watcher by the Way
To the young and the unladen,
To the boy and to the maiden,
"God be with you both to-day.
First your song came ringing,
Now you come, you two,—
Knowing naught of what you do,
Or of what your dreams are bringing.

"O you children who go singing
To the Town down the River,
Where the millions cringe and shiver,
Tell me what you know to-day;
Tell me how far you are going,
Tell me how you find your way.
O you children who go dreaming,
Tell me what you dream to-day."

"He is old and we have heard him,"
Said the boy then to the maiden;

"He is old and heavy laden
With a load we throw away.
Care may come to find us,
Age may lay us low;
Still, we seek the light we know,
And the dead we leave behind us.

"Did he think that he would blind us
Into such a small believing
As to live without achieving,
When the lights have led so far?
Let him watch or let him wither,—
Shall he tell us where we are?
We know best who go together,
Downward, onward, and so far."

II

Said the Watcher by the Way
To the fiery folk that hastened,
To the loud and the unchastened,
"You are strong, I see, to-day.
Strength and hope may lead you

To the journey's end,—
Each to be the other's friend
If the Town should fail to need you.

"And are ravens there to feed you
In the Town down the River,
Where the gift appalls the giver
And youth hardens day by day?
O you brave and you unshaken,
Are you truly on your way?
And are sirens in the River,
That you come so far to-day?

"You are old, and we have listened,"
Said the voice of one who halted;
"You are sage and self-exalted,
But your way is not our way.
You that cannot aid us
Give us words to eat.
Be assured that they are sweet,
And that we are as God made us.

[7]

"Not in vain have you delayed us,
Though the River still be calling
Through the twilight that is falling
And the Town be still so far.
By the whirlwind of your wisdom
Leagues are lifted as leaves are;
But a king without a kingdom
Fails us, who have come so far."

III

Said the Watcher by the Way
To the slower folk who stumbled,
To the weak and the world-humbled,
"Tell me how you fare to-day.
Some with ardor shaken,
All with honor scarred,
Do you falter, finding hard
The far chance that you have taken?

"Or, do you at length awaken
To an antic retribution,
Goading to a new confusion
The drugged hopes of yesterday?

O you poor mad men that hobble,
Will you not return, or stay?
Do you trust, you broken people,
To a dawn without the day?"

"You speak well of what you know not,"
Muttered one; and then a second:
"You have begged and you have beckoned,
But you see us on our way.
Who are you to scold us,
Knowing what we know?
Jeremiah, long ago,
Said as much as you have told us.

"As we are, then, you behold us:
Derelicts of all conditions,
Poets, rogues, and sick physicians,
Plodding forward from afar;
Forward now into the darkness
Where the men before us are;
Forward, onward, out of grayness,
To the light that shone so far."

[9]

IV

Said the Watcher by the Way
To some aged ones who lingered,
To the shrunken, the claw-fingered,
"So you come for me to-day."—
"Yes, to give you warning;
You are old," one said;
"You have old hairs on your head,
Fit for laurel, not for scorning.

"From the first of early morning
We have toiled along to find you;
We, as others, have maligned you,
But we need your scorn to-day.
By the light that we saw shining,
Let us not be lured alway;
Let us hear no River calling
When to-morrow is to-day."

"But your lanterns are unlighted
And the Town is far before you:
Let us hasten, I implore you,"
Said the Watcher by the Way.

"Long have I waited,
Longer have I known
That the Town would have its own,
And the call be for the fated.

"In the name of all created,
Let us hear no more, my brothers;
Are we older than all others?
Are the planets in our way?"—
"Hark," said one; "I hear the River,
Calling always, night and day."—
"Forward, then! The lights are shining,"
Said the Watcher by the Way.

AN ISLAND

(Saint Helena, 1821)

Take it away, and swallow it yourself.
Ha! Look you, there's a rat.
Last night there were a dozen on that shelf,
And two of them were living in my hat.
Look! Now he goes, but he'll come back—
Ha? But he will, I say . . .
Il reviendra-z-à Pâques,
Ou à la Trinité . . .
Be very sure that he'll return again;
For said the Lord: Imprimis, we have rats,
And having rats, we have rain.—
So on the seventh day
He rested, and made Pain.
—Man, if you love the Lord, and if the Lord
Love liars, I will have you at your word
And swallow it. *Voilà.* Bah!

Where do I say it is
That I have lain so long?
Where do I count myself among the dead,

As once above the living and the strong?
And what is this that comes and goes,
Fades and swells and overflows,
Like music underneath and overhead?
What is it in me now that rings and roars
Like fever-laden wine?
What ruinous tavern-shine
Is this that lights me far from worlds and wars
And women that were mine?
Where do I say it is
That Time has made my bed?
What lowering outland hostelry is this
For one the stars have disinherited?

An island, I have said:
A peak, where fiery dreams and far desires
Are rained on, like old fires:
A vermin region by the stars abhorred,
Where falls the flaming word
By which I consecrate with unsuccess
An acreage of God's forgetfulness,
Left here above the foam and long ago
Made right for my duress;

[13]

Where soon the sea,
My foaming and long-clamoring enemy,
Will have within the cryptic, old embrace
Of her triumphant arms—a memory.
Why then, the place?
What forage of the sky or of the shore
Will make it any more,
To me, than my award of what was left
Of number, time, and space?

And what is on me now that I should heed
The durance or the silence or the scorn?
I was the gardener who had the seed
Which holds within its heart the food and fire
That gives to man a glimpse of his desire;
And I have tilled, indeed,
Much land, where men may say that I have planted
Unsparingly my corn—
For a world harvest-haunted
And for a world unborn.

Meanwhile, am I to view, as at a play,
Through smoke the funeral flames of yesterday,

And think them far away?

Am I to doubt and yet be given to know

That where my demon guides me, there I go?—

An island? Be it so.

For islands, after all is said and done,

Tell but a wilder game that was begun,

When Fate, the mistress of iniquities,

The mad Queen-spinner of all discrepancies,

Beguiled the dyers of the dawn that day,

And even in such a curst and sodden way

Made my three colors one.

—So be it, and the way be as of old:

So be the weary truth again retold

Of great kings overthrown

Because they would be kings, and lastly kings alone.

Fling to each dog his bone.

Flags that are vanished, flags that are soiled and furled,

Say what will be the word when I am gone:

What learned little acrid archive men

Will burrow to find me out and burrow again,—

But all for naught, unless

To find there was another Island. . . . Yes,

There are too many islands in this world,
There are too many rats, and there is too much rain.
So three things are made plain
Between the sea and sky:
Three separate parts of one thing, which is Pain . . .
Bah, what a way to die!—
To leave my Queen still spinning there on high,
Still wondering, I dare say,
To see me in this way . . .
Madame à sa tour monte
Si haut qu'elle peut monter—
Like one of our Commissioners . . . *ai! ai!*
Prometheus and the women have to cry,
But no, not I . . .
Faugh, what a way to die!

But who are these that come and go
Before me, shaking laurel as they pass?
Laurel, to make me know
For certain what they mean:
That now my Fate, my Queen,
Having found that she, by way of right reward,
Will after madness go remembering,

And laurel be as grass,—
Remembers the one thing
That she has left to bring.
The floor about me now is like a sward
Grown royally. Now it is like a sea
That heaves with laurel heavily,
Surrendering an outworn enmity
For what has come to be.

But not for you, returning with your curled
And haggish lips. And why are you alone?
Why do you stay when all the rest are gone?
Why do you bring those treacherous eyes that reek
With venom and hate the while you seek
To make me understand?—
Laurel from every land,
Laurel, but not the world?

Fury, or perjured Fate, or whatsoever,
Tell me the bloodshot word that is your name
And I will pledge remembrance of the same
That shall be crossed out never;

Whereby posterity

May know, being told, that you have come to me,

You and your tongueless train without a sound,

With covetous hands and eyes and laurel all around,

Foreshowing your endeavor

To mirror me the demon of my days,

To make me doubt him, loathe him, face to face.

Bowed with unwilling glory from the quest

That was ordained and manifest,

You shake it off and wish me joy of it?

Laurel from every place,

Laurel, but not the rest?

Such are the words in you that I divine,

Such are the words of men.

So be it, and what then?

Poor, tottering counterfeit,

Are you a thing to tell me what is mine?

Grant we the demon sees

An inch beyond the line,

What comes of mine and thine?

A thousand here and there may shriek and freeze,

Or they may starve, in fine.

The Old Physician has a crimson cure

For such as these,

And ages after ages will endure

The minims of it that are victories.

The wreath may go from brow to brow,

The state may flourish, flame, and cease;

But through the fury and the flood somehow

The demons are acquainted and at ease,

And somewhat hard to please.

Mine, I believe, is laughing at me now

In his primordial way,

Quite as he laughed of old at Hannibal,

Or rather at Alexander, let us say.

Therefore, be what you may,

Time has no further need

Of you, or of your breed.

My demon, irretrievably astray,

Has ruined the last chorus of a play

That will, so he avers, be played again some day;

And you, poor glowering ghost,

Have staggered under laurel here to boast

Above me, dying, while you lean

In triumph awkward and unclean,
About some words of his that you have read?
Thing, do I not know them all?
He tells me how the storied leaves that fall
Are tramped on, being dead?
They are sometimes: with a storm foul enough
They are seized alive and they are blown far off
To mould on islands.—What else have you read?
He tells me that great kings look very small
When they are put to bed;
And this being said,
He tells me that the battles I have won
Are not my own,
But his—howbeit fame will yet atone
For all defect, and sheave the mystery:
The follies and the slaughters I have done
Are mine alone,
And so far History.
So be the tale again retold
And leaf by clinging leaf unrolled
Where I have written in the dawn,
With ink that fades anon,
Like Cæsar's, and the way be as of old.

Ho, is it you? I thought you were a ghost.

Is it time for you to poison me again?

Well, here's our friend the rain,—

Mironton, mironton, mirontaine . . .

Man, I could murder you almost,

You with your pills and toast.

Take it away and eat it, and shoot rats.

Ha! there he comes. Your rat will never fail,

My punctual assassin, to prevail—

While he has power to crawl,

Or teeth to gnaw withal—

Where kings are caged. Why has a king no cats?

You say that I'll achieve it if I try?

Swallow it?—No, not I . . .

God, what a way to die!

CALVERLY'S

We go no more to Calverly's,
For there the lights are few and low;
And who are there to see by them,
Or what they see, we do not know.
Poor strangers of another tongue
May now creep in from anywhere,
And we, forgotten, be no more
Than twilight on a ruin there.

We two, the remnant.   All the rest
Are cold and quiet.   You nor I,
Nor fiddle now, nor flagon-lid,
May ring them back from where they lie.
No fame delays oblivion
For them, but something yet survives:
A record written fair, could we
But read the book of scattered lives.

There'll be a page for Leffingwell,
And one for Lingard, the Moon-calf;
And who knows what for Clavering,
Who died because he couldn't laugh?

Who knows or cares? No sign is here,
No face, no voice, no memory;
No Lingard with his eerie joy,
No Clavering, no Calverly.

We cannot have them here with us
To say where their light lives are gone,
Or if they be of other stuff
Than are the moons of Ilion.
So, be their place of one estate
With ashes, echoes, and old wars,—
Or ever we be of the night,
Or we be lost among the stars.

LEFFINGWELL

I—THE LURE

No, no,—forget your Cricket and your Ant,
For I shall never set my name to theirs
That now bespeak the very sons and heirs
Incarnate of Queen Gossip and King Cant.
The case of Leffingwell is mixed, I grant,
And futile seems the burden that he bears;
But are we sounding his forlorn affairs
Who brand him parasite and sycophant?

I tell you, Leffingwell was more than these;
And if he prove a rather sorry knight,
What quiverings in the distance of what light
May not have lured him with high promises,
And then gone down?—He may have been deceived;
He may have lied,—he did; and he believed.

II—THE QUICKSTEP

The dirge is over, the good work is done,
All as he would have had it, and we go;
And we who leave him say we do not know

How much is ended or how much begun.
So men have said before of many a one;
So men may say of us when Time shall throw
Such earth as may be needful to bestow
On you and me the covering hush we shun.

Well hated, better loved, he played and lost,
And left us; and we smile at his arrears;
And who are we to know what it all cost,
Or what we may have wrung from him, the buyer?
The pageant of his failure-laden years
Told ruin of high price.   The place was higher.

III—REQUIESCAT

We never knew the sorrow or the pain
Within him, for he seemed as one asleep—
Until he faced us with a dying leap,
And with a blast of paramount, profane,
And vehement valediction did explain
To each of us, in words that we shall keep,
Why we were not to wonder or to weep,
Or ever dare to wish him back again.

[25]

He may be now an amiable shade,
With merry fellow-phantoms unafraid
Around him—but we do not ask.   We know
That he would rise and haunt us horribly,
And be with us o' nights of a certainty.
Did we not hear him when he told us so?

CLAVERING

I say no more for Clavering
  Than I should say of him who fails
To bring his wounded vessel home
  When reft of rudder and of sails;

I say no more than I should say
  Of any other one who sees
Too far for guidance of to-day,
  Too near for the eternities.

I think of him as I should think
  Of one who for scant wages played,
And faintly, a flawed instrument
  That fell while it was being made;

I think of him as one who fared,
  Unfaltering and undeceived,
Amid mirages of renown
  And urgings of the unachieved;

I think of him as one who gave
  To Lingard leave to be amused,

And listened with a patient grace
  That we, the wise ones, had refused;

I think of metres that he wrote
  For Cubit, the ophidian guest:
"What Lilith, or Dark Lady" . . . Well,
  Time swallows Cubit with the rest.

I think of last words that he said
  One midnight over Calverly:
"Good-by—good man." He was not good;
  So Clavering was wrong, you see.

I wonder what had come to pass
  Could he have borrowed for a spell
The fiery frantic indolence
  That made a ghost of Leffingwell;

I wonder if he pitied us
  Who cautioned him till he was gray
To build his house with ours on earth
  And have an end of yesterday;

[28]

I wonder what it was we saw
    To make us think that we were strong;
I wonder if he saw too much,
    Or if he looked one way too long.

But when were thoughts or wonderings
    To ferret out the man within?
Why prate of what he seemed to be,
    And all that he might not have been?

He clung to phantoms and to friends,
    And never came to anything.
He left a wreath on Cubit's grave.
    I say no more for Clavering.

LINGARD AND THE STARS

The table hurled itself, to our surprise,
At Lingard, and anon rapped eagerly:
"When earth is cold and there is no more sea,
There will be what was Lingard. Otherwise,
Why lure the race to ruin through the skies?
And why have Leffingwell, or Calverly?"—
"I wish the ghost would give his name," said he;
And searching gratitude was in his eyes.

He stood then by the window for a time,
And only after the last midnight chime
Smote the day dead did he say anything:
"Come out, my little one, the stars are bright;
Come out, you lælaps, and inhale the night."
And so he went away with Clavering.

PASA THALASSA THALASSA

"The sea is everywhere the sea."

I

Gone—faded out of the story, the sea-faring friend I remember?
Gone for a decade, they say: never a word or a sign.
Gone with his hard red face that only his laughter could wrinkle,
Down where men go to be still, by the old way of the sea.

Never again will he come, with rings in his ears like a pirate,
Back to be living and seen, here with his roses and vines;
Here where the tenants are shadows and echoes of years uneventful,
Memory meets the event, told from afar by the sea.

Smoke that floated and rolled in the twilight away from the chimney
Floats and rolls no more.   Wheeling and falling, instead,
Down with a twittering flash go the smooth and inscrutable swallows,
Down to the place made theirs by the cold work of the sea.

Roses have had their day, and the dusk is on yarrow and worm-
wood—
Dusk that is over the grass, drenched with memorial dew;
Trellises lie like bones in a ruin that once was a garden,
Swallows have lingered and ceased, shadows and echoes are all.

II

Where is he lying to-night, as I turn away down to the valley,
Down where the lamps of men tell me the streets are alive?
Where shall I ask, and of whom, in the town or on land or on
water,
News of a time and a place buried alike and with him?

Few now remain who may care, nor may they be wiser for
caring,
Where or what manner the doom, whether by day or by night;
Whether in Indian deeps or on flood-laden fields of Atlantis,
Or by the roaring Horn, shrouded in silence he lies.

Few now remain who return by the weed-weary path to his
cottage,
Drawn by the scene as it was—met by the chill and the change;
Few are alive who report, and few are alive who remember,
More of him now than a name carved somewhere on the sea.

"Where is he lying?" I ask, and the lights in the valley are
    nearer;
Down to the streets I go, down to the murmur of men.
Down to the roar of the sea in a ship may be well for another—
Down where he lies to-night, silent, and under the storms.

MOMUS

"Where's the need of singing now?"—
Smooth your brow,
Momus, and be reconciled,
For King Kronos is a child—
Child and father,
Or god rather,
And all gods are wild.

"Who reads Byron any more?"—
Shut the door,
Momus, for I feel a draught;
Shut it quick, for some one laughed.—
"What's become of
Browning?   Some of
Wordsworth lumbers like a raft?

"What are poets to find here?"—
Have no fear:
When the stars are shining blue
There will yet be left a few
Themes availing—
And these failing,
Momus, there'll be you.

UNCLE ANANIAS

His words were magic and his heart was true,
  And everywhere he wandered he was blessed.
Out of all ancient men my childhood knew
  I choose him and I mark him for the best.
Of all authoritative liars, too,
  I crown him loveliest.

How fondly I remember the delight
  That always glorified him in the spring;
The joyous courage and the benedight
  Profusion of his faith in everything!
He was a good old man, and it was right
  That he should have his fling.

And often, underneath the apple-trees,
  When we surprised him in the summer time,
With what superb magnificence and ease
  He sinned enough to make the day sublime!
And if he liked us there about his knees,
  Truly it was no crime.

All summer long we loved him for the same
    Perennial inspiration of his lies;
And when the russet wealth of autumn came,
    There flew but fairer visions to our eyes—
Multiple, tropical, winged with a feathery flame,
    Like birds of paradise.

So to the sheltered end of many a year
    He charmed the seasons out with pageantry
Wearing upon his forehead, with no fear,
    The laurel of approved iniquity.
And every child who knew him, far or near,
    Did love him faithfully.

THE WHIP

The doubt you fought so long,
The cynic net you cast,
The tyranny, the wrong,
The ruin, they are past;
And here you are at last,
Your blood no longer vexed.
The coffin has you fast,
The clod will have you next.

But fear you not the clod,
Nor ever doubt the grave:
The roses and the sod
Will not forswear the wave.
The gift the river gave
Is now but theirs to cover:
The mistress and the slave
Are gone now, and the lover.

You left the two to find
Their own way to the brink;
Then—shall I call you blind?—

You chose to plunge and sink.
God knows the gall we drink
Is not the mead we cry for,
Nor was it, I should think—
For you—a thing to die for.

Could we have done the same,
Had we been in your place?—
This funeral of your name
Throws no light on the case.
Could we have made the chase,
And felt then as you felt?—
But what's this on your face,
Blue, curious, like a welt?

There were some ropes of sand
Recorded long ago,
But none, I understand,
Of water. Is it so?
And she—she struck the blow,
You but a neck behind. . .
You saw the river flow—
Still, shall I call you blind?

THE WHITE LIGHTS

(BROADWAY, 1906)

When in from Delos came the gold
That held the dream of Pericles,
When first Athenian ears were told
The tumult of Euripides,
When men met Aristophanes,
Who fledged them with immortal quills—
Here, where the time knew none of these,
There were some islands and some hills.

When Rome went ravening to see
The sons of mothers end their days,
When Flaccus bade Leuconoë
To banish her Chaldean ways,
When first the pearled, alembic phrase
Of Maro into music ran—
Here there was neither blame nor praise
For Rome, or for the Mantuan.

When Avon, like a faery floor,
Lay freighted, for the eyes of One,

With galleons laden long before
By moonlit wharves in Avalon—
Here, where the white lights have begun
To seethe a way for something fair,
No prophet knew, from what was done,
That there was triumph in the air.

EXIT

For what we owe to other days,
Before we poisoned him with praise,
May we who shrank to find him weak
Remember that he cannot speak.

For envy that we may recall,
And for our faith before the fall,
May we who are alive be slow
To tell what we shall never know.

For penance he would not confess,
And for the fateful emptiness
Of early triumph undermined,
May we now venture to be kind.

LEONORA

They have made for Leonora this low dwelling in the ground,
And with cedar they have woven the four walls round.
Like a little dryad hiding she'll be wrapped all in green,
Better kept and longer valued than by ways that would have
been.

They will come with many roses in the early afternoon,
They will come with pinks and lilies and with Leonora soon;
And as long as beauty's garments over beauty's limbs are
thrown,
There'll be lilies that are liars, and the rose will have its own.

There will be a wondrous quiet in the house that they have made,
And to-night will be a darkness in the place where she'll be laid;
But the builders, looking forward into time, could only see
Darker nights for Leonora than to-night shall ever be.

THE WISE BROTHERS

First Voice

So long adrift, so fast aground,
What foam and ruin have we found—
    We, the Wise Brothers?
Could heaven and earth be framed amiss,
That we should land in fine like this—
    We, and no others?

Second Voice

Convoyed by what accursed thing
Made we this evil reckoning—
    We, the Wise Brothers?
And if the failure be complete,
Why look we forward from defeat—
    We, and what others?

Third Voice

Blown far from harbors once in sight,
May we not, going far, go right,—
    We, the Wise Brothers?
Companioned by the whirling spheres,
Have we no more than what appears—
    We, and all others?

BUT FOR THE GRACE OF GOD

"There, but for the grace of God, goes . . ."
    There is a question that I ask,
        And ask again:
    What hunger was half-hidden by the mask
        That he wore then?

    There was a word for me to say
        That I said not;
    And in the past there was another day
        That I forgot:

    A dreary, cold, unwholesome day,
        Racked overhead,—
    As if the world were turning the wrong way,
        And the sun dead:

    A day that comes back well enough
        Now he is gone.
    What then? Has memory no other stuff
        To seize upon?

Wherever he may wander now
    In his despair,
Would he be more contented in the slough
    If all were there?

And yet he brought a kind of light
    Into the room;
And when he left, a tinge of something bright
    Survived the gloom.

Why will he not be where he is,
    And not with me?
The hours that are my life are mine, not his,—
    Or used to be.

What numerous imps invisible
    Has he at hand,
Far-flying and forlorn as what they tell
    At his command?

What hold of weirdness or of worth
    Can he possess,
That he may speak from anywhere on earth
    His loneliness?

Shall I be caught and held again
    In the old net?—
He brought a sorry sunbeam with him then,
    But it beams yet.

FOR ARVIA

ON HER FIFTH BIRTHDAY

You Eyes, you large and all-inquiring Eyes,
That look so dubiously into me,
And are not satisfied with what you see,
Tell me the worst and let us have no lies:
Tell me the meaning of your scrutinies,
And of myself. Am I a Mystery?
Am I a Boojum—or just Company?
What do you say? What do you think, You Eyes?

You say not; but you think, beyond a doubt;
And you have the whole world to think about,
With very little time for little things.
So let it be; and let it all be fair—
For you, and for the rest who cannot share
Your gold of unrevealed awakenings.

THE SUNKEN CROWN

Nothing will hold him longer—let him go;
Let him go down where others have gone down;
Little he cares whether we smile or frown,
Or if we know, or if we think we know.
The call is on him for his overthrow,
Say we; so let him rise, or let him drown.
Poor fool! He plunges for the sunken crown,
And we—we wait for what the plunge may show.

Well, we are safe enough. Why linger, then?
The watery chance was his, not ours. Poor fool!
Poor truant, poor Narcissus out of school;
Poor jest of Ascalon; poor king of men.—
The crown, if he be wearing it, may cool
His arrogance, and he may sleep again.

DOCTOR OF BILLIARDS

Of all among the fallen from on high,
We count you last and leave you to regain
Your born dominion of a life made vain
By three spheres of insidious ivory.
You dwindle to the lesser tragedy—
Content, you say.   We call, but you remain.
Nothing alive gone wrong could be so plain,
Or quite so blasted with absurdity.

You click away the kingdom that is yours,
And you click off your crown for cap and bells;
You smile, who are still master of the feast,
And for your smile we credit you the least;
But when your false, unhallowed laugh occurs,
We seem to think there may be something else.

SHADRACH O'LEARY

O'Leary was a poet—for a while:
He sang of many ladies frail and fair,
The rolling glory of their golden hair,
And emperors extinguished with a smile.
They foiled his years with many an ancient wile,
And if they limped, O'Leary didn't care:
He turned them loose and had them everywhere,
Undoing saints and senates with their guile.

But this was not the end.   A year ago
I met him—and to meet was to admire:
Forgotten were the ladies and the lyre,
And the small, ink-fed Eros of his dream.
By questioning I found a man to know—
A failure spared, a Shadrach of the Gleam.

HOW ANNANDALE WENT OUT

"They called it Annandale—and I was there
To flourish, to find words, and to attend:
Liar, physician, hypocrite, and friend,
I watched him; and the sight was not so fair
As one or two that I have seen elsewhere:
An apparatus not for me to mend—
A wreck, with hell between him and the end,
Remained of Annandale; and I was there.

"I knew the ruin as I knew the man;
So put the two together, if you can,
Remembering the worst you know of me.
Now view yourself as I was, on the spot—
With a slight kind of engine. Do you see?
Like this . . . You wouldn't hang me? I thought not."

ALMA MATER

He knocked, and I beheld him at the door—
A vision for the gods to verify.
"What battered ancientry is this," thought I,
"And when, if ever, did we meet before?"
But ask him as I might, I got no more
For answer than a moaning and a cry:
Too late to parley, but in time to die,
He staggered, and lay shapeless on the floor.

When had I known him? And what brought him here?
Love, warning, malediction, hunger, fear?
Surely I never thwarted such as he?—
Again, what soiled obscurity was this:
Out of what scum, and up from what abyss,
Had they arrived—these rags of memory?

MINIVER CHEEVY

Miniver Cheevy, child of scorn,
   Grew lean while he assailed the seasons;
He wept that he was ever born,
   And he had reasons.

Miniver loved the days of old
   When swords were bright and steeds were prancing;
The vision of a warrior bold
   Would set him dancing.

Miniver sighed for what was not,
   And dreamed, and rested from his labors;
He dreamed of Thebes and Camelot,
   And Priam's neighbors.

Miniver mourned the ripe renown
   That made so many a name so fragrant;
He mourned Romance, now on the town,
   And Art, a vagrant.

Miniver loved the Medici,
   Albeit he had never seen one;

He would have sinned incessantly
    Could he have been one.

Miniver cursed the commonplace
    And eyed a khaki suit with loathing;
He missed the mediæval grace
    Of iron clothing.

Miniver scorned the gold he sought,
    But sore annoyed was he without it;
Miniver thought, and thought, and thought,
    And thought about it.

Miniver Cheevy, born too late,
    Scratched his head and kept on thinking;
Miniver coughed, and called it fate,
    And kept on drinking.

THE PILOT

From the Past and Unavailing
Out of cloudland we are steering:
After groping, after fearing,
Into starlight we come trailing,
And we find the stars are true.
Still, O comrade, what of you?
You are gone, but we are sailing,
And the old ways are all new.

For the Lost and Unreturning
We have drifted, we have waited;
Uncommanded and unrated,
We have tossed and wandered, yearning
For a charm that comes no more
From the old lights by the shore:
We have shamed ourselves in learning
What you knew so long before.

For the Breed of the Far-going
Who are strangers, and all brothers,
May forget no more than others

Who looked seaward with eyes flowing.

But are brothers to bewail

One who fought so foul a gale?

You have won beyond our knowing,

You are gone, but yet we sail.

VICKERY'S MOUNTAIN

Blue in the west the mountain stands,
   And through the long twilight
Vickery sits with folded hands,
   And Vickery's eyes are bright.

Bright, for he knows what no man else
   On earth as yet may know:
There's a golden word that he never tells,
   And a gift that he will not show.

He dreams of honor and wealth and fame,
   He smiles, and well he may;
For to Vickery once a sick man came
   Who did not go away.

The day before the day to be,
   "Vickery," said the guest,
"You know as you live what's left of me—
   And you shall know the rest.

"You know as you live that I have come
   To this we call the end.

No doubt you have found me troublesome,
　　But you've also found a friend;

"For we shall give and you shall take
　　The gold that is in view;
The mountain there and I shall make
　　A golden man of you.

"And you shall leave a friend behind
　　Who neither frets nor feels;
And you shall move among your kind
　　With hundreds at your heels.

"Now this that I have written here
　　Tells all that need be told;
So, Vickery, take the way that's clear,
　　And be a man of gold."

Vickery turned his eyes again
　　To the far mountain-side,
And wept a tear for worthy men
　　Defeated and defied.

Since then a crafty score of years
    Have come, and they have gone;
But Vickery counts no lost arrears,
    He lingers and lives on.

Blue in the west the mountain stands,
    Familiar as a face.
Blue, but Vickery knows what sands
    Are golden at its base.

He dreams and lives upon the day
    When he shall walk with kings.
Vickery smiles—and well he may.
    The life-caged linnet sings.

Vickery thinks the time will come
    To go for what is his;
But hovering, unseen hands at home
    Will hold him where he is.

There's a golden word that he never tells
    And a gift that he will not show.
All to be given to some one else—
    And Vickery not to know.

BON VOYAGE

Child of a line accurst
 And old as Troy,
Bringer of best and worst
 In wild alloy—
Light, like a linnet first,
 He sang for joy.

Thrall to the gilded ease
 Of every day,
Mocker of all degrees
 And always gay,
Child of the Cyclades
 And of Broadway—

Laughing and half divine
 The boy began,
Drunk with a woodland wine
 Thessalian:
But there was rue to twine
 The pipes of Pan.

Therefore he skipped and flew
    The more along,
Vivid and always new
    And always wrong,
Knowing his only clew
    A siren song.

Careless of each and all
    He gave and spent:
Feast or a funeral
    He laughed and went,
Laughing to be so small
    In the event.

Told of his own deceit
    By many a tongue,
Flayed for his long defeat
    By being young,
Lured by the fateful sweet
    Of songs unsung—

Knowing it in his heart,
    But knowing not

The secret of an art
　　That few forgot,
He played the twinkling part
　　That was his lot.

And when the twinkle died,
　　As twinkles do,
He pushed himself aside
　　And out of view:
Out with the wind and tide,
　　Before we knew.

THE COMPANION

Let him answer as he will,
Or be lightsome as he may,
Now nor after shall he say
Worn-out words enough to kill,
Or to lull down by their craft,
Doubt, that was born yesterday,
When he lied and when she laughed.

Let him find another name
For the starlight on the snow,
Let him teach her till she know
That all seasons are the same,
And all sheltered ways are fair,—
Still, wherever she may go,
Doubt will have a dwelling there.

ATHERTON'S GAMBIT

The master played the bishop's pawn,
For jest, while Atherton looked on;
The master played this way and that,
And Atherton, amazed thereat,
Said "Now I have a thing in view
That will enlighten one or two,
And make a difference or so
In what it is they do not know."

The morning stars together sang
And forth a mighty music rang—
Not heard by many, save as told
Again through magic manifold
By such a few as have to play
For others, in the Master's way,
The music that the Master made
When all the morning stars obeyed.

Atherton played the bishop's pawn
While more than one or two looked on;
Atherton played this way and that,
And many a friend, amused thereat,

Went on about his business
Nor cared for Atherton the less;
A few stood longer by the game,
With Atherton to them the same.

The morning stars are singing still,
To crown, to challenge, and to kill;
And if perforce there falls a voice
On pious ears that have no choice
Except to urge an erring hand
To wreak its homage on the land,
Who of us that is worth his while
Will, if he listen, more than smile?

Who of us, being what he is,
May scoff at others' ecstasies?
However we may shine to-day,
More-shining ones are on the way;
And so it were not wholly well
To be at odds with Azrael,—
Nor were it kind of any one
To sing the end of Atherton.

FOR A DEAD LADY

No more with overflowing light
Shall fill the eyes that now are faded,
Nor shall another's fringe with night
Their woman-hidden world as they did.
No more shall quiver down the days
The flowing wonder of her ways,
Whereof no language may requite
The shifting and the many-shaded.

The grace, divine, definitive,
Clings only as a faint forestalling;
The laugh that love could not forgive
Is hushed, and answers to no calling;
The forehead and the little ears
Have gone where Saturn keeps the years;
The breast where roses could not live
Has done with rising and with falling.

The beauty, shattered by the laws
That have creation in their keeping,
No longer trembles at applause,

Or over children that are sleeping;
And we who delve in beauty's lore
Know all that we have known before
Of what inexorable cause
Makes Time so vicious in his reaping.

TWO GARDENS IN LINNDALE

Two brothers, Oakes and Oliver,
Two gentle men as ever were,
Would roam no longer, but abide
In Linndale, where their fathers died,
And each would be a gardener.

"Now first we fence the garden through,
With this for me and that for you,"
Said Oliver.—"Divine!" said Oakes,
"And I, while I raise artichokes,
Will do what I was born to do."

"But this is not the soil, you know,"
Said Oliver, "to make them grow:
The parent of us, who is dead,
Compassionately shook his head
Once on a time and told me so."

"I hear you, gentle Oliver,"
Said Oakes, "and in your character
I find as fair a thing indeed

[68]

As ever bloomed and ran to seed
Since Adam was a gardener.

"Still, whatsoever I find there,
Forgive me if I do not share
The knowing gloom that you take on
Of one who doubted and is done:
For chemistry meets every prayer."

"Sometimes a rock will meet a plough,"
Said Oliver; "but anyhow
'Tis here we are, 'tis here we live,
With each to take and each to give:
There's no room for a quarrel now.

"I leave you in all gentleness
To science and a ripe success.
Now God be with you, brother Oakes,
With you and with your artichokes:
You have the vision, more or less."

"By fate, that gives to me no choice,
I have the vision and the voice:

Dear Oliver, believe in me,
And we shall see what we shall see;
Henceforward let us both rejoice."

"But first, while we have joy to spare
We'll plant a little here and there;
And if you be not in the wrong,
We'll sing together such a song
As no man yet sings anywhere."

They planted and with fruitful eyes
Attended each his enterprise.
"Now days will come and days will go,
And many a way be found, we know,"
Said Oakes, "and we shall sing, likewise."

"The days will go, the years will go,
And many a song be sung, we know,"
Said Oliver; "and if there be
Good harvesting for you and me,
Who cares if we sing loud or low?"

They planted once, and twice, and thrice,
Like amateurs in paradise;

And every spring, fond, foiled, elate,
Said Oakes, "We are in tune with Fate:
One season longer will suffice."

Year after year 'twas all the same:
With none to envy, none to blame,
They lived along in innocence,
Nor ever once forgot the fence,
Till on a day the Stranger came.

He came to greet them where they were,
And he too was a Gardener:
He stood between these gentle men,
He stayed a little while, and then
The land was all for Oliver.

'Tis Oliver who tills alone
Two gardens that are now his own;
'Tis Oliver who sows and reaps
And listens, while the other sleeps,
For songs undreamed of and unknown.

'Tis he, the gentle anchorite,
Who listens for them day and night;

But most he hears them in the dawn,
When from his trees across the lawn
Birds ring the chorus of the light.

He cannot sing without the voice,
But he may worship and rejoice
For patience in him to remain,
The chosen heir of age and pain,
Instead of Oakes—who had no choice.

'Tis Oliver who sits beside
The other's grave at eventide,
And smokes, and wonders what new race
Will have two gardens, by God's grace,
In Linndale, where their fathers died.

And often, while he sits and smokes,
He sees the ghost of gentle Oakes
Uprooting, with a restless hand,
Soft, shadowy flowers in a land
Of asphodels and artichokes.

[72]

THE REVEALER

(Roosevelt)

He turned aside to see the carcase of the lion: and behold, there was a swarm of bees and honey in the carcase of the lion. . . . And the men of the city said unto him, What is sweeter than honey? and what is stronger than a lion?—*Judges*, 14.

The palms of Mammon have disowned
The gift of our complacency;
The bells of ages have intoned
Again their rhythmic irony;
And from the shadow, suddenly,
'Mid echoes of decrepit rage,
The seer of our necessity
Confronts a Tyrian heritage.

Equipped with unobscured intent
He smiles with lions at the gate,
Acknowledging the compliment
Like one familiar with his fate;
The lions, having time to wait,
Perceive a small cloud in the skies,
Whereon they look, disconsolate,
With scared, reactionary eyes.

A shadow falls upon the land,—
They sniff, and they are like to roar;
For they will never understand
What they have never seen before.
They march in order to the door,
Not knowing the best thing to seek,
Nor caring if the gods restore
The lost composite of the Greek.

The shadow fades, the light arrives,
And ills that were concealed are seen;
The combs of long-defended hives
Now drip dishonored and unclean;
No Nazarite or Nazarene
Compels our questioning to prove
The difference that is between
Dead lions—or the sweet thereof.

But not for lions, live or dead,
Except as we are all as one,
Is he the world's accredited
Revealer of what we have done;

What you and I and Anderson
Are still to do is his reward;
If we go back when he is gone—
There is an Angel with a Sword.

He cannot close again the doors
That now are shattered for our sake;
He cannot answer for the floors
We crowd on, or for walls that shake;
He cannot wholly undertake
The cure of our immunity;
He cannot hold the stars, or make
Of seven years a century.

So Time will give us what we earn
Who flaunt the handful for the whole,
And leave us all that we may learn
Who read the surface for the soul;
And we'll be steering to the goal,
For we have said so to our sons:
When we who ride can pay the toll,
Time humors the far-seeing ones.

Down to our nose's very end
We see, and are invincible,—
Too vigilant to comprehend
The scope of what we cannot sell;
But while we seem to know as well
As we know dollars, or our skins,
The Titan may not always tell
Just where the boundary begins.

THE MAN WHO DIED TWICE
(1924)

To James Earle Fraser
and
Laura Gardin Fraser

THE MAN WHO DIED TWICE

If I had not walked aimlessly up town
That evening, and as aimlessly walked back,
My glance had not encountered then, if ever,
The caps and bonnets of a singing group
That loudly fought for souls, and was at first
No more than a familiar spot of sound
And color in a long familiar scene;
And even at that, if an oblique persuasion
Had not withheld me and inveigled me
To pause, I should have passed as others did,
Never to guess that while I might have touched him,
Fernando Nash was beating a bass drum
And shouting Hallelujah with a fervor
At which, as I remember, no man smiled.

Not having seen him for so many years,
And seeing him now almost as one not there
Save in remembrance or imagination,
I made of his identity, once achieved,

[1]

The ruin of a potential world-shaker—
For whom the world, which had for twenty years
Concealed him and reduced him, had not shaken.
Here were the features, and to some degree
The massive aggregate of the whole man,
Where former dominance and authority
Had now disintegrated, lapsed, and shrunken
To an inferior mystery that had yet
The presence in defeat. At a first view,
He looked a penitent Hercules, none too long
Out of a hospital. But seeing him nearer,
One read where manifest havoc must for years
Have been at work. What havoc, and what work,
I partly guessed; for I had known before
That he had always been, apart from being
All else he was, or rather along with it,
The marked of devils—who must have patiently
And slowly crucified, for subtle sport,
This foiled initiate who had seen and felt
Meanwhile the living fire that mortal doors
For most of us hold hidden. This I believe,
Though some, with more serenity than assurance,
May smile at my belief and wish me well.

Puzzled, I waited for a word with him;
And that was how I came to know all this
That I should not have known, so he averred,
But for a memory that survived in him
That I had never yelped at him with others,
Who feared him, and was not among the biters,
Who, in the years when he was dangerous
Had snapped at him until he disappeared
Into the refuge of remoter streets
And partly was forgiven. I was grateful—
Assuring him, as adroitly as I might,
That had he written me down among the biters,
I should have mourned his error. "Let them go;
They were so near forgotten," he said once,
Up there in his gaunt hall-room not long after,
"That memory now becomes a punishment
For nourishing their conceit with my contempt
As once I did. What music have they made
So different in futility since then
That one should hear of it? I make a music
That you can hear all up and down Broadway.
Glory to God! Mine are the drums of life—
After those other drums. I had it—once.

They knew I had it, and they hated me
For knowing just what they had. I had it—once!"
At that his eyes glowed and his body shook,
And it was time to go. Fernando Nash,
I saw, would not be long in going farther.
The rough resentful egoist I had known
Was now a shell. The giant had been reduced;
And the old scorn that once had been his faith
Was now a sacrificial desperation.

A year before I found him in the street
Pounding a drum and shouting for the lost,
He had for a long time, from his account,
Inhabited the Valley of the Shadow—
A region where so many become so few
To know, that each man there believes himself
In his peculiar darkness more alone
Than any other. However that may have been,
Fernando Nash's darkness we may grant
Was dark enough, and as peculiar, surely,
As all those who had bitten him would have had it.
I was not one of them, though I fear now
That acquiescence was a larger part

Than he conceived in me of kindliness;
And I should not have thought him outwardly
Much given to soliciting, in those days,
Attention any softer than respect—
Which was not always, or by those who feared him,
Conferred without a sure and small alloy
Of hate, that made the giver and gift alike
A negligible mildew to Fernando,
In whose equipment of infirmities
A place that might have held a little envy
Was overfilled with scorn. Out of his realm,
And only with a tinkler's apprehension
Of what those unproved opuses of his
Were like to do when they began to sing,
There was no reason in eternity
For me to be distressed at his assurance
That they were all immortal. Who was I,
A hewer of wood, to say that they were not,
Or to be disaffected if they should be?
To-day I cannot tell you what was in them,
Nor shall to-morrow know; for they are now,
As ashes, mute as ashes. Whether he found
Their early glory to be going out,

Or whether in one last fury against fate
He made an end of them, as afterwards
He would have made an end of other relics,
I do not know. The most he ever told me
Later about them was that they were dead,
And how they died, and how much better it was
For them to be where dead things ought to be—
Adding at once, that I be not mistaken,
That he had known himself to be no liar
The while he praised them. It was not for them
That he fed scorn to envy in those days,
Nor out of them so much as out of him
That envy grew. "They knew I had it—once,"
He said; and with a scowl said it again,
Like a child trying twice the bitter taste
Of an unpalatable medicine;
"They knew I had it—once! Do you remember
What an upstanding Ajax I was then?
And what an eye I had? I scorched 'em with it.
I scared 'em; and they knew I was a giant
I knew it, also; and if I had known
One other thing, I should have gone down then
Upon my knees for strength—I who believed

Myself to be secure. They knew a little,
But they knew nothing of what I know now.
A year before you found what's left of me,
That evening in the street, I should have said
My way was blank and ruinous to the end,
But there was more to be, Glory to God!
There was to be a more revealing end
Than that—an end that once had been for me
The bitterest end of all—and is not so.
For in the music I have heard since then
There are the drums of life. Glory to God!
I had it—once."

                    So much of him was gone,
That I would hear no more. All the way home,
The restive exultation in his eyes
And in his bearing, altered and subdued,
Was like that of a dead friend out of hell,
Humbled, and hardly more than half assured
Of even his respite. There may have been a giant,
If he must have it so, but where was now
The man whom I remembered and was once
Fernando Nash? So much of him was gone,
That I should never learn, from what remained,

The story of the rest—or so I thought,
All the way home. But there was more concealed
Within the shell of him than I supposed—
More than I know to-day; though many a time
Thereafter I went back to him again,
Till I had heard enough to make me doubt
The use of doubting, for he had it—once.
I had known that, and then for years had lost him—
For all those years while he had crushed unripe
The grapes of heaven to make a wilder wine
Than earth gives even to giants who are to live
And still be giants. It may be well for men
That only few shall have the grapes of heaven
To crush. The grapes of heaven are golden grapes,
And golden dregs are the worst dregs of all—
Or so Fernando surely would have said
A year before.

        A year before I found him,
Pounding a drum and shouting to the street,
Fernando Nash heard clocks across the town
One midnight, and was forty-five years old;
And he was too far sundered from his faith
And his ambition, buried somewhere together

Behind him to go stumbling back for them,
Only to find a shadowy grave that held
So little and so much. The barren room—
The same in which I sought him a year later—
Was not much larger than the iron bed
On which he sat; and all there was of music
About the place was in a dusty box
Of orchestrations for the janitor,
And in the competent plain face of Bach,
Calm in achievement, looking down at him
Like an incurious Titan at a worm,
That once in adolescent insolence
Would have believed himself another Titan.
Fernando sat with his large heavy face
Held forward in his hands and cursed his works
Till malediction was a weariness,
And all his makeshift insolence a lie
That only cravens who had trained themselves
To fight and had not fought were silly enough
To fancy for the truth. No insolence
That he remembered would have been sufficient
Without additions and foreseen betrayals
To make of him this penitential emblem

Of that which he was not. When he had called
Himself a worm, another worm turned at once
Within his heart and bit him; and just then
The candid face of one that heretofore
Had been for him as near to the divine
As any might be, and through all had remained so,
Became as if alive there on the wall,
Transfigured into living recognition,
Wherein there was much wonder and some pity,
And more regret. The Titan, it would seem,
For the first time, and ruinously too late,
And only for a moment interested,
Saw what had happened and could do no more,
Having seen, than to recede ineffably
Aloft into the distance and the dark,
Until he was as high as a large star
That shines on death and life and death in life
Indifferently. Fernando Nash at length
Arose, leaving his bed for his one chair;
And under the sick gleam of one gas-flame,
That had for years to shadowy lodgers given
More noise than light, he sat before a glass
That was more like a round malevolent eye

Filmed with too many derelict reflections,
Appraising there a bleared and heavy face
Where sodden evil should have been a stranger.

"What are you doing here? And who are you?"
He mumbled, with a cloudy consciousness
Of having felt a ghostly blow in the face
From an unseemly mirrored visitor
That he had not invited. "And how long
Have you been on your way, do you suppose,
To come to this? If I remember you
As first you were anointed and ordained,
There was a daemon in you, not a devil,
Who told you then that when you heard those drums
Of death, it would be death to follow them.
You were to trust your daemon and to wait,
And wait, and still to wait. You had it—once.
You had it then—though you had not yet heard it,
Coming as it would have to come some time,
Blown down by choral horns out of a star
To quench those drums of death with singing fire
Unfelt by man before. You knew it then.
You felt it singing down out of the sky

When you were only a small boy at school;
And you knew then that it was all for you,
For you and for the world, that it was coming.
Where is it now? It may be coming yet,
For someone else, but you do not know that;
And that was not what you were meant to know.
O, you poor toad, why could you not have waited?
Why did you have to kill yourself like this?
Why did you let the devil's retinue
That was to be a part be everything,
And so defeat your daemon till your star
Should sing unheard for you whose ears were left
Only for drums and songs of your destroyers?
And now even they are gone—all but the drums.
You knew that if you waited, they, not you,
Should cease—that they should all be hushed at last
In that great golden choral fire of sound.
'Symphony Number Three. Fernando Nash.'
Five little words, like that, if you had waited,
Would be enough to-night, you flabby scallion,
To put you on the small roll of the mighty.
As for the other two, they're in a box
Under the bed; and they will soon be nowhere.

You do not have to mourn now over them,
For they were only ladders carrying you
Up to the half-way place from which you fell,
And should have fallen, since you were going to fall,
A little faster, and so broken at once
Your neck. Why could you not have fallen faster
And saved yourself all this? If you had given
The devil a sign to play those drums of death
Longer and louder at about that time,
You might be now a carrion more at ease
Than you are like to be till you make haste.
What else, in God's name, are you waiting for?
And where's the use? And while I'm asking that;
Where was the use of all your prentice-years
Wherein you toiled, while others only tinkled,
Till you were master of a new machine
That only your invention could have built
Or driven? You built it and you let it rust.
A fog of doubt that a small constant fire
Would have defeated had invisibly
And imperceptibly crept into it,
And made the miracle in it that was yours
A nameless toy for the first imbecile

To flout who found it—wherefore he'll not find it.
Presently Number One and Number Two
Will be beyond all finding. Number Three
Will not be farther from his eyes to-morrow;
And they'll all be as safe together then
As we should be if we had not been born.
The circle fills itself; and there you are
Inside it, where you can't crawl out of it.
It holds you like a rat in a round well,
Where he has only time and room to swim
In a ring until he disappears and drowns.
If it be true that rats abandon ships
That sail away to sink, praise be to rats!
If you were one, you'd never find another
For shipmate. He would know you for a fool,
And therefore dangerous. You're not even a rat;
For a good rat will wait for what is coming,
Whether it comes or not. You could not wait,
Knowing that it must come. You had it—once.
You had enough of it to make you know,
And were among the sceptred of the few
In having it. But where's your sceptre now?
You threw it away; and then went wallowing

After that other music, and those drums—
Assured by more than man's authority
That all you had not then was only waiting
To make of that which once was you a torch
Of sound and fire that was to flood the world
With wonder, and overwhelm those drums of death
To a last silence that should have no death.
That would have been somewhat the way of it,
You somewhat less than eminent dead fish,
If you had waited and had been content
To let those devils and those devil-women
Beat as they would your drums and dance and sing
And be invisible. You had followed them,
And seen and heard enough of them, God knows,
Already. Your daemon had a lenience then,
And you had not the protest of a soul
Between you and your right to stay alive;
All which was as it was. But it was so
No longer when you knew it was not so,
And that one day a bush might bloom with fire
At any trivial hour of inattention,
Whereafter your employment would have been
A toil of joy for immortality.

Your drums of death, from which it all began,
Would then have been illusions most enduring
When most entirely and divinely dead;
And you, Fernando Nash, would now have been—
But who's alive to know that you're alive
To care?   Look at that burned out face of yours,
You bloated greasy cinder, and say who.
Say who's to care, and then say, if you will,
Why anyone in a world where there's a cockroach,
Should care for you.   You insufficient phoenix
That has to bake at last in his own ashes—
You kicked out, half-hatched bird of paradise
That had to die before you broke your shell,—
Who cares what you would be if you had flown?
A bird that men are never to see flying,
Or to hear singing, will not hold them long
Away from less ethereal captivations;
Just as a fabulous and almighty fish
That never swam to sight will hardly be
For long the unsighted end of their pursuit.
Why do you make then such a large ado
Over such undefended evidence?
You fat and unsubstantial jelly-fish,

That even your native ocean has disowned
And thrown ashore, why should men ask or care
What else you would have been if you had waited?
You crapulous and overgrown sick lump
Of failure and premeditated ruin,
What do you think you are—one of God's jokes?
You slunk away from him, still adequate
For his immortal service, and you failed him;
And you knew all the while what you were doing.
You damned yourself while you were still alive.
You bulk of nothing, what do you say to that?
You paramount whale of lust and drunkenness,
You thing that was, what do you say to that?"

No man so near to glory as he was once
Was ever, I fancied, quite so inglorious
As in his penance—which is here somewhat
Softened in deference to necessity—
Fernando Nash revealed himself to me
In passionate reminiscence a year later.
Occasional strokes, at least, among the many
That I had counted must have registered
Luxurious and unmerited flagellation,

Wherein abasement was akin to pride,
If not a part of it.   No man so mired
As he was in his narrative, I told him,
Could have such choral gold poured down from heaven
When he was young. But there he shook his head
In hopeless pity—not for the doomed, I saw,
But rather for the sanguine ordinary
That has no devil and so controls itself,
Having nothing in especial to control.

"Hewers of wood," I said, "and drawers of water
Will always in their innocence be insisting
That your enamel of unrighteousness
Is too thick to be real."   In his changed eyes,
Where the old fire was gone, there was almost
The coming of a smile: "How do you know?"
He answered, asking.   "What have you done to know?
Where have you been that you should think you know?
Do you remember when I told you once
That every sleeve of genius hides a knife
That will, if necessary, carve a way
Through snakes and oxen? Most that I said then
Has gone with all the rest, but I keep this

As a memorial of my retribution.
I wonder if a notion has yet seized you
To bury the keenest sword you ever saw
For twenty years in mud, and then go back
To find what may be left of it.   If not,
You need not.   Save your curiosity
Two decades of unprofitable conjecture,
And look at me.   Look at Fernando Nash,—
The heir-apparent of a throne that's ashes,
The king who lost his crown before he had it,
And saw it melt in hell."

                          When he had ceased
I could almost have heard those drums of death
Pounding him on to a defeated grave,
Which, had I not by chance encountered him
Beating another drum for the Lord's glory
There in the street, would have been no man's grave,
Like that of one before him who still wears
The crown he could not lose.   I thought of him,
Whose tomb was an obscure and stormy legend,
Sure of how little he had cared for that—

And how much less would this man here have cared
Whether he found a nameless grave, or no grave,
So long as he had left himself alive
Behind him in a world that would have loved him
Only the more for being out of it.
That long orchestral onslaught of redemption
Would have exonerated flesh and folly
And been his everlasting epitaph—
Which time would then have read as variously
As men are various in their ways and means
Of reading. That would have cancelled everything,
And all his earthly debts—or left him willing
To pay them peradventure as they might
Or must be paid. But they had run too long.
His birthright, signed away in fettered sloth
To the most ingenious and insatiable
Of usurers, had all vanished; and the more
He might have been a king, the more their greed
Would mock him and his tatters, and abase him;
And his vituperative temporizing
Over a soul in rags would mend no holes.
"But there's a crown that even the lowliest
May learn to wear," he said. "Glory to God!"

And his eyes glittered with an icy joy
That made me hope that he was wearing it.
"Of course we can't forget," he said in answer
To doubt that in my silence may have spoken;
"Yet there is much that we may leave behind,
And there is always more if we go on."

In marking after that the accuracy
Of his minute recount, I found it hard
Not to believe that he remembered all—
Save that which of itself was everything,
Or once had been so. There before the mirror,
That bitter midnight when he heard the clocks,
There was not much forgetting; and since then
Only one year was gone. Before that glass
He must have sat for more than a long hour,
Hurling the worst of his vocabulary
At his offending image. "Now you have learned
A part of what you are," he told his face,
"And you may say whatever occurs to you
As an addendum. You deficient swine,
Where do you see the best way out of it?

You are not crazy enough to cut your throat;
You are not solid enough to shoot yourself.
There's always water, but you don't like that;
And you're not sure enough of what might happen
If you should inadvertently have swallowed
A few small pills. But there's another way—
A longer and a more monotonous one,
Yet one that has no slight ascendency
Over the rest; for if you starve to death,
Maybe the God you've so industriously
Offended in most ways accessible
Will tell you something; and if you live again
You may attain to fewer discrepancies
In less within you that you may destroy.
That's a good way for you to meet your doubt,
And show at the same time a reverence
That's in you somewhere still." And I believe,
Though he may well then have believed in nothing
More real than a defective destiny,
That it was in him somewhere, as he said.
There was a fervor in his execration
That was not only drama; though I question
Whether I should have found him and his drum

That evening a year after, in the street,

If he had not gone farther, while he starved,

Into the valley—which had for twenty years

Already beguiled and held him. What had been

Without this uncompanioned expiation,

I do not know, and I might never have known.

The shape of one more foiled obscurity

Might some time as a cadaver have ensured

A massive and unusual exhibition

Of God's too fallible image—and no more.

Though some had wondered idly, and they might,

Why the defeated features of a giant

Should have been moulded so imperiously

To be the mask of frailty in oblivion,

None would have rated such a scrapped utensil

As more than common, or uncommon, waste;

None would have guessed what violent fire had once,

In such a cracked abandoned crucible,

Fused with inseparable obscure alloy

Celestial metal, which would else have been

The fabric of a seething instrument

That might have overflowed with other fire

Brought falling from ethereal distances.

It might, I say, cleaving inveterately
To my conviction that in this man's going
More went than when in Venice went the last
Authentic wizard, who in his house of sound
Hears not the siege of Time. Failing a way
To prove that one obscure evangelist,
Beating a drum and shouting for the Lord,
Not only might have been (to fill again
That weary sieve with wine) but was in fact
A giant among fewer than half your fingers
Of Jubal's clan, only his mark on me
Will now avail me for the confirmation
Of more, I fear, than the confirmable—
As he would have foretold. Reverting quaintly
And incompatibly with his arrogance
To the weak stings of his inferiors,
And even while dying, he smiled. "Poor souls," he said,
"That are born damned, although they may be feared
May be forgiven, though hated, and then hanged;
Whereas my early colleagues, had they known
How soon and surely I was to damn myself,
Not only would have ceased their fearing me,
But would have loved me—seeing that I was doomed.

That midnight—when I cursed myself so long—
Roundly and rightly, be it well understood—
There came a few revealing memories
That set me then to wondering just what soft
And anaesthetic language of affection
They would have brought for me if they had known
How far I was from all that formerly
Had for so long offended and oppressed them.
Poor children!—and they might all have been happy
If in the place of misapplied creation
A more discriminate wisdom had supplied
Discrimination—and some humility
Before God's few that are in spite of us
Surviving, somehow." And all this to me
Was not quite so irrelevant as to others
It may at first appear; for the same thought
Pursued me always in those other days
When I had harmonized ingeniously
Some brief and unoffending cerebration
Which, had it been one, would have been a song.
To some persuasion sharper than advice
I must have yielded slowly and at last
Let fall my lyre into the fearsome well

Of truth, hearing no protest from below;
Thereby surviving bitterness to indite
This tale of one who foundered in a slough
More fearsome, and lost there a mightier lyre.

He was not humble, this Fernando Nash;
Yet while he may have ministered on occasion
To a discreet humility in others,
I doubt if in the scorn he flung to us,
Mostly in silence, his preoccupation
Saw crumbs of any nurture less assuaging
Than wholesome and unfrosted honesty;
Albeit his arrogance may have merited
The few vindictive nippings that amazed
As much as they annoyed, and would have seemed
Allegiance, had their negligible venom
Been isolated from another virus,
Which later was to be a leprosy
Of self-contempt attending revelation.

When he had heard the last stroke of those clocks,
And called himself again the last hard name
That his abundant lexicon released,

He tore those two initial symphonies
Into as many pieces of oblivion
As he had reasons, or believed he had,
After those empty years, for their extinction.
"They were so 'temerarious' and 'exotic'
When they were written twenty years ago,"
He said, "that all who saw them laughed at them—
Not seeing with me that they would be to-day
About as temerarious and exotic
As Händel's hat. They were good harbingers,
But were they living they would not be mine;
They were not what it was that I was doing
The while I did them. Many, if they were theirs,
Would eat their ears for joy, but they're not theirs,
Or mine. Glory to God, they're nowhere now.
They were not mine; they were not yet the vintage;
Though I should have enjoyed, when I was young,
The taste of them. But they were not the wine
To fill my cup, and now it doesn't matter."

There was for some time an obscurity
For me in such a reasoning, but I learned,

And I have striven loyally to believe
That he did well—sure that he did not well
In going down those dark stairs again that night
For the beginning of a last debauch
That was to be a prelude, as he put it,
Wincing in reminiscence, for a fugue
Of ravening miseries and recriminations
Assembling in remorseful exposition
That was to be remorseless and infernal
Before they were devouring one another
In a malicious fantasy more infernal,
And richer in dissonance and involution
Than all his dreams together had heretofore
Aspired or dared to be.   When half-way down
The second of those four forbidding stairways,
He heard those drums again, and on his face
He felt with more resentment than alarm
A touch of warning, like a chilly wind
Within a tomb.   "You are too late," he said,
Holding his heavy jaws harder together;
"And you have come too many times before."
Then he went grimly down and out of doors,
And was alone there in a lonely street

That led where soon he might not be so lonely,
Or so severe in his particulars.

After three weeks that would have relegated
A village blacksmith or a stevedore
Of mortal average to a colder sleep
Than has a waking, he awoke one day
Late in the afternoon, miraculously
In bed again and wondering, as before,
How this time he had got there. Looking up,
He met the face of Bach upon the wall,
Who bowed at him, gravely but not unkindly;
And he, not yet alive to what was coming,
And not to be defective in attention
To a great master, bowed acknowledgment;
Whereat the salutations were repeated,
And there was a preparatory silence,
Heavy with strangeness and expectancy,
Which would have been a monitory dread—
But for the master's nod of satisfaction
And interest in the coming through a keyhole
Of a slow rat, equipped with evening dress,
Gold eye-glasses, and a conductor's wand,

Soon followed by a brisk and long procession
Of other rats, till more than seventy of them,
All dressed in black and white, and each of them
Accoutred with his chosen instrument,
Were ranged in order on the footworn carpet
That lay between Fernando and the door.
Having no chairs, they stood erect and ready,
And having made obeisance to the master
Upon the wall, who signified his pleasure,
And likewise to the man upon the bed,
They played with unforeseen solemnity
The first chords of the first rat symphony
That human ears had heard.   Baffled and scared,
Fernando looked at Bach, who nodded slowly,
And, as he fancied, somewhat ominously;
And still the music sounded, weird but firm,
And the more fearful as it forged along
To a dark and surging climax, which at length
Broke horribly into coarse and unclean laughter
That rose above a groaning of the damned;
And through it all there were those drums of death,
Which always had been haunting him from childhood.
Without a formal ending, or any sign

That there was ever to be an end, the rats
Danced madly to the long cacophony
They made, and they made faces at Fernando
The while they danced—till one of them, the leader,
Bowed mockingly, and vanished through the keyhole,
As he had come; and after him went others,
Each with a leering courtesy as he went,
Till more than seventy of them disappeared,
Leaving their auditor lying there alone
In a cold sweat, while his impassive master
Frowned, shook his head, and was again a picture.

Fernando Nash, deploring afterwards
This innovation of orchestral rats
As a most arbitrary intermezzo
Between the sordid prelude that was over
And the infernal fugue that was to come,
Smiled wearily, and shrugged his heavy shoulders,
Like one who would be glad to say no more,
Yet must relate the rest to somebody
Before he died. Somebody might believe him;
And it was I, who had not bitten him

(Achilles' heel was never to be cured),
Who might, if anyone might, believe him now,
And say to others that he was not mad
Through that incessant week of lonely torture
Which no food would have eased, and through the days
That followed while he starved indomitably,
With a cold hope that his long-punished heart
Would after time be still.   Day after day,
And endless night following endless night,
There were those miseries and recriminations
Devouring one another but never dead,
Until one afternoon he lay remembering
The day when those unusual visitors
Had made a more unusual music for him,
And having made it mocked him and departed.
Again he looked up at the face of Bach,
Considering wearily, with a bleak regret
How far those features in their dusty frame
Were now from seeing that there was in this world
So frail a relic as Fernando Nash,
And how much farther still they were from caring,
With more than common care, could they have seen him.
Could they have seen him they would not have known

What fires had burned in that cadaverous ruin
Below them, or what hopes, or what remorse,
Or what regret.   For a long time he lay
Aware of action hardly in a finger,
But with a coming wonder of surprise
For a new clearness which had late begun
To pierce forbidden chambers long obscured
Within him, and abandoned, being so dark
And empty that he would not enter them—
Fearful of what was not there to be found
Should he go there to see.   They might be dark,
But folly that made them so had kept them so,
Like an indulgent slayer who binds a wound
That he has washed with a lethargic poison,
And waits at ease with his malignity
For stagnant fury to accumulate
A mortal sloth within—and in so far
As that was in a manner merciful,
Though now it seemed there was to be an end
Of even that mercy.   After grateful darkness,
There was to be the pain of seeing too clearly
More than a man so willing to see nothing
Should have to see.

                              Still motionless, he lay there
Laboring to persuade a lying hope
That this new clarity was the light that comes
Before the night comes, and would not last long—
Yet knowing that it was not. Like shining grain,
Long fouled and hidden by chaff and years of dust
In a dark place, and after many seasons
Winnowed and cleaned, with sunlight falling on it,
His wits were clear again. He had no power
To use them, and at first repudiated
The faintest wakening flicker of any wish
For use of any such power. But a short fight
Found his whole fragile armor of negation
So tattered that it fell away from him
Like time-worn kingly rags of self-delusion
At the rough touch of the inevitable—
Till he confessed a rueful willingness
To reason that with time and care this power
Would come, and coming might be used. He smiled
And closed his eyes, finding an awkward humor
In such an unforeseen enfranchisement
From such a long and thwarting servitude.
A calm that all his life had been a stranger

To the confusions that were born with him
Composed and overpowered him as he felt,
Enveloping and persuading body and brain
Together, a cool relief as if warm wings
Were in the air above him. So there he lay,
Without a motion or a wish to move,
And with a sense of having only to rise
And give his hands to life. A grateful shame
For all his insults to the Holy Ghost
That were forgiven was like an anodyne
Laid on a buried wound somewhere within him,
Deeper than surgeons go; and a vast joy,
Which broke and swept and covered him like a sea
Of innocence, leaving him eager as a child
That has outlived experience and remembers
Only the golden moment as it flows,
Told him in silence that was more than speech
That after passion, arrogance and ambition,
Doubt, fear, defeat, sorrow and desperation,
He had wrought out of martyrdom the peace
That passeth understanding. Still he lay there
Smiling to think how soon those burrowing teeth
Which he had felt within him for so long

Would cease their famished gnawing at his heart
Which after all the many prolonged assaults
It had survived was toiling loyally,
With only an uncertain fire to drive it;
And still he would not move. There would be time
For all things in their order. He was hungry—
Hungry beyond a longer forced endurance,
But in this new unwillingness not to live,
No longer forced, there was a gratefulness
Of infinite freedom and humility,
After a bondage of indignant years
And evil sloth; and there was in this calm,
Which had unlooked for been so long in coming,
A balanced wealth of debts and benefits
Vaster than all ambition or achievement.
Hereafter it would be enough to serve,
And let the chosen shine.

                        So there he lay,
Luxuriating vaguely on the moment
When he should rise and with a blessed effort
Go down those shadowy stairs again for food;

And if in his prevision of that moment
He had not lain so long awaiting it,
Those drums of death might opportunely then
Have stayed an hour the sound of their approach,
Throbbing as always, and intolerably,
Through stifling clouds of sound that hid, like smoke,
Tumultuous and elusive melodies,
Now for so long imprisoned as no longer
To be released. Hearing them first, and faintly,
For once and for once only without flinching,
He smiled and sighed. Let others, if they must,
Hear them and follow them. He was at peace
With them for the first time in recollection,
And willingly for the future would remain so.
At last alive, it was enough to serve,
And so to be content where God should call him;
But there must be no haste. His fires were low,
And too much fuel might yet extinguish them.
At first he must be frugal with his coals,
If only for the peril of too much comfort
Given at once, and without more atonement.
So arrogant in his new humility
Was he becoming, and so chary was he

Of exultation, that to break his fast
With no excess of zeal he planned a fare
That would have saddened Simeon on his pillar;
And he might soon have been in search of it,
Had not another silence, like a blow
That somehow stunned him to clairvoyant awe,
Held him as if mysterious hands had bound him
With cords he could not see. Now he could hear
Those drums again, and they were coming nearer,
Still muffled within the same unyielding cloud
Of sound and fire, which had somewhere within it
A singing flame that he might not for long
Endure, should such a mocking hour as this
Be the one hour of all when after years
Of smouldering it should leap at him and scorch him.
He felt his fingers clutching hungrily
At nothing, as the fingers of one drowning
Would clutch at seaweed floating where he sank;
And he could feel the pounding of those drums
Like iron upon the fibre of his brain.
His feeble heart was leaping, and a cold
Invisible hand was heavy on his throat—
As if in mercy, if it need be so,

To strangle him there before he knew too soon
What he must know too late.

                              Now it was fear,
Not peace, that falling on him like a wave,
Covered and overwhelmed him; it was fear,
Not peace, that made him cold and left him trembling
After the cold had passed.   The coming drums
Were like the vanguard of a Juggernaut
Approaching slowly through a rolling cloud
Of fiery sound that was anon to burst
And inundate him with an ecstasy
Of mad regret before those golden wheels
Behind should crush him.   He could only wait,
Therefore, and in his helplessness be seared
With his own lightning.   When the music leapt
Out of that fiery cloud and blinded him,
There would be recognition for a moment,
And then release.   So his prophetic fancy,
Smiting him with deceit, foresaw the blow,
Not seeing what other shafts of doom and mercy
There are from which an injured God may choose
The one or many that in his exigence

His leisure may affect.   Seldom it is
The mightier moments of necessity
That we can see are coming come to us
As we have seen them.   Better or worse for us,
Anticipation waits upon surprise;
And though Fernando Nash in his exhaustion
Prayed now for that cold hand upon his throat
To close and have it over, no cold hand
Was there to close.   Now there was nothing for him
But to lie still and hear those coming drums,
Muffled as always in a smoky cloud
Of burning sound that in a moment more
Would burst above him into flaming rain
That once he would have welcomed on his knees,
Unspeakably; and so he might have done
Could he have waited with his inner doors
Unbarred to the celestial messengers
Who may have come and gone a score of times,
Only to find again, and still again,
That he was absent on another journey
Into the dismal valley of the shadow
That was to be his home.   But that was over.
They had not found him then.   He had not waited.

Failing a willingness to be assured
That in so doing he would have left by now
The worst of a light burden far behind him
And found the rest to be Olympian gold,
He had impawned it all for mouldy pottage.

Telling me that, he sighed and shut his teeth,
And with a mortal smile shook his large head
At me before he went back to those drums.
They were not going to sound, as it appeared,
Their long approach for ever, but were soon
To cease, and only intermittently
Be heard again till choral gold came down
Out of a star to quench and vanquish them
With molten glory.   Trembling there alone,
He knew that there would now be falling on him
The flaming rain he feared, or the one shaft
Of singing fire that he no longer feared—
At which that hand might close upon his throat
Till in oblivion there might then be peace;
And so at first there was—if there be peace
In the complete oblivion of achievement.

Instead of bursting as he prayed it might,
And ending him with one destroying blast
Of unendurable fulfilment, slowly
And imperceptibly that cloud of sound
Became a singing mist, which, having melted,
Revealed a fire that he had always felt,
But never known before.   No lightning shaft
Of blinding and immediate dissolution
Was yet impending: there was only joy,
And a vast wonder that all this had been
So near him for so long. Smiling and still,
He listened gratefully. It had come at last;
And those far sent celestial messengers
That he had for so long a time denied
Had found him now. He had offended them,
He had insulted and forsaken them,
And he was not forsaken. They had come,
And in their coming had remembered only
That they were messengers, who like himself
Had now no choice; and they were telling him this
In the last language of mortality,
Which has no native barrier but the grave.
Now it was theirs to sing and his to wear

The glory, although there was a partnership
Somewhere that a surviving grace in him
Remembered; for though the star from which they came
Shone far within the dark infinity
That was himself, he had not made it shine—
Albeit he may have wrought more notably
Than might another for its extinguishment.

But there was time for not much more of that
Than a bewildered smile of acquiescence.
The quivering miracle of architecture
That was uprising lightly out of chaos,
And out of all the silence under time,
Was a gay temple where the Queen of Life
And her most loyal minions were protracting
Melodious and incessant festival
To the least lenient of divinities.
Joy, like an infinite wine, was everywhere,
Until it proved itself at last a languor,
Now less engrossed with festive pageantry
Than with an earth-born sensuous well-being
Which in the festive pageant was divine.
Of all the many of those who danced and sang

And celebrated, there was none to note
A silent entrance of the most abhorred
And oldest of all uninvited strangers—
A lean and slinking mute with a bassoon,
Who seized attention when a languid hush
Betrayed a perilous rift of weariness
Where pleasure was not joy, and blew a tune
Of hollow triumph on a chilly reed
From which all shrank. The tumult after that
Was an unprized expenditure of beauty
Awaiting doom. It was awaiting also
The faint approach of slow, infernal drums
That were not long in coming, bringing with them
A singing horde of demons, men and women,
Who filled the temple with offensive yells
And sang to flight the frightened worshippers.

Fearing to think, he lay as one secure
So long as he lay motionless. If he moved
It might be only to plunge down again
Into a more chaotic incoherence
And a more futile darkness than before.
There was no need of moving, and no need

Of asking; for he knew, as he had known

For years, unheard, that passionate regret

And searching lamentation of the banished,

Who in abandoned exile saw below them

The desecrated lights of a domain

Where they should walk no more. Inaudible

At first, he knew it only as a presence

Intangible, but he knew that it was there;

And as it went up slowly to the stars

Carrying all the sorrow of man with it,

He trembled that he should so long have been

So near to seizing immortality.

Well, here it was. And while he might have died

If it had ceased, he would have been as one

Who cared no more, having had everything,

Where there was no more caring. But he knew

That he was not yet dead, and that the rest

Would soon be coming. When the voices fell,

He knew that through them he should hear those drums

Again, but he was not afraid of them.

They were his drums, and the far sound of riot

Below there in the gloom was also his.

It was all his to give. "Poor fool," he thought;

"Praise God you are a fool, and call it yours."
And he lay tranquil through another silence.

Though he condemned the specious tyranny
Of illustrations and explicit schemes,
He kept in his creative charnel house
More pictures hidden of the dead and dying
Than men should see; and there were these among them,
Which he submitted once, reluctantly,
As to a loyal friend who would forgive them,
And then forget.   Yet I remember now
That in the place of languid folly flown
To mourn apart, bereft of its illusions,
The desolation of its realities,
There woke amid the splendors that were lost
A frantic bacchanale of those usurpers,
Who in affronting life with evil rites
Of death, knew not themselves to be the dead—
In false authority mistaking riot
And scorn for power, and hell for paradise.
Intoxicated by their swift invasion
Whereafter conquest was an easy trifle,
And hating the magnificence they cursed,

Seeing not the beauty or the use of it,
They soiled with earthy feet the shining floor
Flinging the dregs of their debaucheries
From crystal cups against the gleaming walls
Of Life's immortal house. Too ignorant
Of where they were to be afraid to know,
They shrieked and sang in shrill delirium
With vicious ecstasy for louder drums—
Till, crowning insolence with infamy,
They must have wearied God—who, pitying them,
Smote with avenging trumpets into silence
All but those drums of death, which, played by **Death**
Himself, were beating sullenly alone.

They ceased, and after stillness in which time
And space, together perishing, were no more
To him than indecisions that were gone,
Far off there was a murmur and a stirring
Of liberation, and a marching hymn
Sang of a host returning.   All the banished
Who had been driven from the house of life
To wander in the valley of the shadow
Were sounding as they came in chastened order

The praise of their deliverance and return.
A singing voice that gathered and ascended
Filled the vast dome above them till it glowed
With singing light that seemed at first eternal,
But was at first not so.   There were those drums
Again, to frustrate with a last intrusion
The purifying and supreme festival
Of life that had returned and in its house
Was daring to be free.   But freedom wavered
Out of the voices that were praising it;
And while it wavered, the lean hand of Death
Beat with a desperate malevolence,
More sinister in its evil emptiness
Than when that carnal chorus of the dead
With corybantic and infatuate glee
Had howled it out of hearing—till once more
There were those golden trumpets, and at last
There was that choral golden overflow
Of sound and fire, which he had always heard—
And had not heard before.   Now it had come,
And had not gone.   Nothing had gone that came.
All he had known and had not waited for
Was his; and having it, he could not wait now.

With blinding tears of praise and of exhaustion
Pouring out of his eyes and over his cheeks,
He groped and tottered into the dark hall,
Crying aloud to God, or man, or devil,
For paper—not for food. It may have been
The devil who heard him first and made of him,
For sport, the large and sprawling obstacle
They found there at the bottom of the stairs.

A fortnight after that, Fernando Nash
Lay contemplating with a special envy
A screen between him and another bed
That would anon be vacant. For some time,
So he had learned, the probabilities
Had seen for him a similar departure,
But seeing indifferently at the last hour
That some residual and peculiar service
Awaited the survival of as much
As was remaining of him to survive,
Had left him and abandoned him again
To life. The fire of personality,
Still glowing within him, drew mysteriously

From those assisting at his resurrection
A friendly patience, and a sort of wonder
That wore a laughing kindness. With a lesion
Like his there would be no more golden fire
Brought vainly by perennial messengers
For one that would no longer recognize them,
Or know that they had come. There were somewhere
Disfigured outlines of a glory spoiled
That hovered unrevealed and unremembered,
But they were like to those of blinding jewels
Wrought beyond earth to value beyond earth,
To be defaced and hammered valueless
By a sick idiot, and insanely sunk
In darker water than where ships go down
Hull-crushed at mid-night. When he told me that,
He may have had a vision of himself
In his last, starless plunge. "Make a swift end
Of what I leave behind," he said to me.
"Burn me to ashes; and when that is done,
Take me somewhere to sea and let me sink,
And fear not for my soul. I have found that,
Though I have lost all else. All but those drums;
And they are but the last hope of the devil.

Mine are the drums of life—and they are mine.
You may not like them.   All I ask of you
Is to believe me when I say to you
That what I had, I had.   It was no dream
That followed me so long, and found me only
To make of me a child that should henceforth
Go into streets and beat the drums of life.
I make a joyful noise unto the Lord,
But I know it's a noise, and the Lord knows it—
Just as he knows that I have told to you
Only the truth, and that I had it—once.
Fool as I was and remnant as I am,
My prayer will be to you that you forget me,
If in your memory there survive a doubt
That I was less than you believed I was
Till I was chastened.   For I swear to you
That as I knew the quality, not slight,
Of a young harvest that I would not save,
I know that in the fields where kings have been
Before me there was never found by them
A sheaf more golden than the grain I lost
When the Lord smote my field that afternoon.
I am not telling you this to salve a bruise,

For now the bruise is healed. I shall go lame
Because of it, but the Lord's ways are strange,
And I am not to suffer; and I believe
The reason for this is that I have not lied.
I have not lied to Him in praising Him,
Nor more to you in praising what He gave me
And in his wisdom took away again.
We cannot measure what the world has lost
Until we know the gauge the builders use
Who made it. All we know about the world
For certain is that it appears to be.
And in so far as I am sure of that
So am I sure that I was once as much
As you believed and others feared I was.
I have not drugged a clamoring vanity
With lies that for a little while may seem
To sweeten truth. There was no need of that;
And God knows now that there is less than ever.
Now I can beat my drum and let those drums
Of death pound as they will. Once, for an hour,
I lived; and for an hour my cup was full
With wine that not a hundred, if a score,
Have tasted that are told in history.

Having it unconfirmed, I might be mad
To-day if a wise God had not been kind,
And given me zeal to serve Him with a means
That you deplore and pardonably distrust.
The dower of ignorance is to distrust
All that it cannot feel, and to be rich
In that which it has not.   I can be rich
In all that I have had, and richer still
In this that I have now.   Glory to God!
Mine are the drums of life, and though I wait
For no more messengers—or for none save one,
Who will be coming soon—I had it, once.
Not more than once or twice, and hardly that,
In a same century will another have it,
To know what I have lost.   You do not know.
I've made for you only a picture of it,
No worse or better than a hundred others
Might be of the same thing—all mostly trash.
But I have found far more than I have lost
And so shall not go mourning.   God was good
To give my soul to me before I died
Entirely, and He was no more than just
In taking all the rest away from me.

I had it, and I knew it; and I failed Him.
I did not wait."

        "You could not wait," I told him,
"Instead of moulding you to suit the rules,
They made you mostly out of living brimstone,
And set you in a somewhat fiery world
Not to be burnt." But there he shook his head
And looked at me as he had looked before,
Like one who was a little sorry for me.
I had made several entrances already
With my determinism, and always failed.
He would have none of it. He was to blame,
And it was only right that he should lose
What he had won too late. "Why pity me?"
He asked, strangely, "You see that I'm content.
I shall not have to be here very long,
And there's not much that I may do for God
Except to praise Him. I shall not annoy you,
Or your misguided pity, with my evangel,
For you must have yours in another dress.
I shall not ask if you believe me wise
In this that I am doing. I do not care.

I'll only ask of you that you believe
What I have told you.   For I had it—once."

To each his own credulity, I say,
And ask as much.   Fernando Nash is dead;
And whether his allegiance to the Lord
With a bass drum was earnest of thanksgiving,
Confusion, penance, or the picturesque,
Is not the story.   There was in the man,
With all his frailties and extravagances,
The caste of an inviolable distinction
That was to break and vanish only in fire
When other fires that had so long consumed him
Could find no more to burn; and there was in him
A giant's privacy of lone communion
With older giants who had made a music
Whereof the world was not impossibly
Not the last note; and there was in him always,
Unqualified by guile and unsubdued
By failure and remorse, or by redemption,
The grim nostalgic passion of the great
For glory all but theirs.   And more than these,
There was the nameless and authentic seal

Of power and of ordained accomplishment—
Which may not be infallibly forthcoming,
Yet in this instance came. So I believe,
And shall, till admonition more disastrous
Than any that has yet imperilled it
Invalidates conviction. Though at first,
And many a time thereafter, my persuasion
May well have paused and halted, I believe
To-day that all he told me for the truth
Was true—as I believed him long ago
To be the giant of his acknowledgment.
Crippled or cursed or crucified, the giant
Was always there, and always will be there.
For reasons less concealed and more sufficient
Than words will ever make them, I believe him
To-day as I believed him while he died,
And while I sank his ashes in the sea.